Maximizing School Guidance Program Effectiveness

A GUIDE FOR ADMINISTRATORS & PROGRAM DIRECTORS

Copyright © 1998 ERIC Counseling and Student
Services Clearinghouse.

ERIC/CASS Publications
School of Education
201 Ferguson Building
University of North Carolina at Greensboro
PO Box 26171
Greensboro, NC 27402-6171

ISBN 1-56109-083-2

This publication was funded by the US Department of
Education, Office of Educational Research and
Improvement, Contract no. RR93002004. Opinions
expressed in this publication do not necessarily reflect the
positions of the US Department of Education, OERI, or
ERIC/CASS.

Table of Contents

Preface

Garry R. Walz

I would be hard pressed to name an area where we have more requests for a book and are unable to do anything about it (because there isn't one!) than a book having to do with developing school guidance programs. It seems almost anyone connected with schools could use such a book. School administrators have dozens of questions about school guidance programs that they can't find answers to. Guidance administrators longingly chat about how useful it would be to have a guide about managing school guidance programs. School Board members have to settle for what people tell them. Counselor educators know a great deal about guidance programs, but even they can't keep up with all the changes. And, if you're a new counselor with a brand spanking new MA in counseling and raring to go, but you have a few questions (maybe a hundred or more?)—well, good luck!

Fact of the matter is, nobody has all the answers or for that matter even knows what questions need to be asked.

That is, nobody did until now. Cass Dykeman has done it. It isn't that he knows more than the rest of us (although he could!), it's just that he got smart about it. He asked others, like school administrators, counselor educators, and experienced counselors, what the real questions were. And he kept asking around until he found somebody to answer each of the questions. It tells you that we weren't far off the mark about how hard it is to find answers; that it took 53 people writing to get the information he wanted. No wonder we've all been looking so long and so hard.

But your search is over! This is it. Trust me. You won't find anything like it and you darn well won't find anything as good as it is.

But, you aren't interested in knowing how hard it was to put it together. You want to know what it will do for you. Plenty! I daresay you will get all your questions answered, even some you didn't even think about.

Just skim the table of contents. The topics are one we are all interested in. And the writers are a pretty respectable bunch as well. So we've got a winner.

For somebody who looks so young, Cass has come up with a book that has a lot of wisdom in it. We're all indebted to you, Cass, and your great stable of writers. And as the Director of ERIC/CASS, I am proud to be able to publish a book that is so practical. Come to think of it, this book will stand out for how helpful a succinct book can be.

Garry R. Walz
Director
Toll free: 1-800-414-9769
Email: ericcass@uncg.edu

Foreword

Cass Dykeman, Editor

It's hard work—being a school administrator these days! You are expected to create better learning environments with decreasing amounts of both money and support. One possible source of greater support for your learning environment improvement goals is your school counselor. Yet, you are a rare school administrator if you have ever had any training on school counseling. Unfortunately, this training gap usually results in school administrators taking a "hands-off" approach with their school counselor. Is this you? A hands-off approach is unfortunate because your leadership is a prime determiner of the extent to which school counselors can serve the promotion of better learning environments.

This ERIC/CASS publication aims to "fill-in" critical gaps in your administrator training on the subject of school counseling. Each article was coauthored by a counselor educator and a school administrator and focuses on a specific topic, such as "The School Counselor's Role With Discipline." All of the authors sought to write practical articles that would help you to become a better leader and consumer of school counseling. Each article was written to stand alone. Thus, this series can be read sequentially or you can pick and choose the articles you want to read.

This publication is a product of the School Counseling Interest Network of the Association for Counselor Education and Student Services (ERIC/CASS) at The University of North Carolina at Greensboro. Garry Walz, Director of ERIC/CASS, strongly supported the idea and was responsilble for its publication.

Garry tells me that Phil Piele, Director of the ERIC

Clearinghouse on Educational Management, felt there was a real need for this publication and gave it his endorsement. So we're off to a good start!

Thank you for your interest in school counseling!

Cass Dykeman, Ph.D., NCC, NCSC, MAC is Associate Professor of Applied Psychology and Director of School Counseling, Eastern Washington University, WA.

Introduction

Why Should School Administrators Care About School Counseling?

Edwin L. Herr

This capsule series is designed to provide a guide to school counseling for school administrators. It addresses a series of topics that describes practices, problems, and processes for which school counselors have expertise and to which their professional education has been directed. In providing these insights about school counseling for administrators, it is hoped that these chapters will address a question that may be implicit as the reader examines the contents of this publication: "Why should school administrators care about school counseling?"

School counselors, like school administrators, have become increasingly professionalized during this century. They bring a level and type of expertise that can contribute to the purposes of the school in unique ways, an expertise often under-estimated in its impact on students and others. They are neither administrators nor teachers in the conventional sense, but they are educators. In addition to their direct assistance to students, they have training and skills that can provide assistance and support to administrators as well as to classroom teachers— but only if their contributions to the purposes of both administrators and teachers are recognized and used effectively.

The skeptical administrator can greet the above notions with a "so-what" reply. Or, instead, he or she may suggest that school counselors should be quasi-administrators or staff members who do all of the paper work related to students, who create the Master Schedule of courses and then take care of all of the logistics of the school testing program, who coordinate all of the IAP meetings for special needs students or other similar tasks that need to be done to maintain school organization and integrity. While school counselors can and often are used in these ways, to do so minimizes the many other contributions that school counselors can make that are of direct service to students and to their educational and personal development. In this context, school administrators should care about school counseling because administrators are the ultimate interpreters to students, parents, and teachers of the importance of school counseling in their school. Administrators will largely determine whether counseling will be trivialized or viewed as an administrative arm of the school, or, instead, be seen as a central factor in the school's mission. Thus, a principal's actions largely determine whether counselors will be seen as minor players in the school's agenda or as professionals who are the primary agents to help students

   (a) develop personal and career aspirations;
   (b) explore and act on goals with planfulness and
        responsibility;
   (c) understand how course work and curriculum options
        can be known and used systematically to facilitate their
        growth and development;
   (d) connect their present academic courses with future
        opportunities that will require such content and skills;
        and
   (e) achieve such goals within a context by which they can
        gain in self-esteem, in confidence, in effective
        interpersonal skills and in academic focus.

School administrators should care about school counseling because it is a school-wide resource, for which they are primarily responsible. What school counselors do is ultimately shaped by the characteristics of the local school, its demographics of student, parent, and teacher needs, and how these are defined and acted on by the principal of the school. In fact, principals, other school administrators, and school counselors should see themselves, and be seen as, members of a guidance team that analyzes needs data and together plans the most effective deployment of guidance resources. This notion was expressed nearly twenty years ago in a joint statement by the American School Counselors Association, the National Association of Secondary School Principals, and the American Association of School Administrators and it still has current value. The statement says, "Principals and counselors share a tremendous responsibility in the process of helping students achieve the maximum benefits from their school experience. An awareness and appreciation of the contribution each can make should enable both principal and counselor to utilize more fully their individual competencies in serving youth" (Costar, 1978, p.9). Such a perspective requires effective and frequent communication between administrators and school counselors about the challenges that each faces, challenges that could be mutually addressed. Administrators and school counselors need to see the school counselor's time, expertise, and skills as a major asset which must be deployed systematically and which is consistent with the priority needs of a particular school at a particular time in its history.

Within such contexts, it is unlikely that there is one model of school counseling that can fit the characteristics and needs of all schools. At given times, the emphases in school counseling will shift from being provided to all students to help with issues of planning and choice of academic courses, curriculum pathways, and postsecondary options, to a focus on selected groups of students whose needs include crisis intervention, support, and behavioral management. In this sense, there is a wide array of ways by which school counseling can be implemented and focused in different schools. In general, the different emphases in the roles of school counselors are captured in the different goals for, and the intended recipients of, three helping processes used by the school counselor: counseling, consulting, and coordination. As described by the American School Counselors Association (1996-1997)

1. Counseling is a complex helping process in which the counselor establishes a confidential working relationship;

2. Consultation is a cooperative process in which the counselor-consultant assists others to think through problems and to develop skills that make them more effective in working

with students;

3. Coordination is a leadership process in which the counselor helps organize and manage a school's counseling program and related services (p. 21). Each of these helping processes can be used on behalf of students or teachers or parents or administrators depending upon the goals to be achieved or the problems to be solved. Regardless of the focus of these helping processes, school counselors are obligated by their ethical standards to treat each person to whom they provide assistance with respect and dignity, without prejudice; to preserve the person's right to self-direction, self-development, choice, and the responsibility for decisions reached; to privacy and to counselor compliance with all laws, policies, and ethical standards pertaining to confidentiality (American School Counselors Association, 1996-97). These processes and these ethical commitments of the school counselor are important contributions to the school's total impact on its various constituencies—concerns about which a school administrator should care deeply.

There are many ways to envision the contributions that counselors make to schools and to students. One of the roles that school counselors can play for many students, and about which school administrators should care, is helping students personalize their education. In a school environment in which there are multiple opportunities for choice of academic content and of behavior, many students find themselves adrift, unsure, unclear of what they are doing in school, what pathways they should be pursuing; and how to make personal meaning out of the smorgasbord of course content and behavioral possibilities from which they are expected to choose. Counselors can provide a sanctuary where students can explore these questions of uncertainty and confusion. Counselors can help students construct individual plans that give them direction and a sense of meaning as they plot their educational pathways. But, they can also do so in ways that reduce information deficits, enhance exploration and increase student feelings of responsibility for who they are, who they want to be, and who they can be. School counseling in such cases can help students to find new meaning and relevance in their academic course work so that they can approach it with greater confidence, and can recognize the connections between academic offerings and their personal goals, not as hurdles to be leaped over, but as tools that help them lay foundations for future academic and career opportunities. In these ways, school counseling can help students to find order, predictability, and significance within otherwise ambiguous academic environments.

Helping students to find meaning in their school work and to make connections between the academic knowledge and skills they are acquiring and their importance in future jobs and post-secondary educational opportunities, is often related to encouraging students to remain in school. School counselors are often cited by students as important influences that help them to choose to remain and graduate rather than be an early school-leaver. The school administrator should care about the importance of school counseling's role in drop-out prevention both from a humane and from a cost-benefit perspective. The humane view is that in a society that is increasing the educational requirements for most jobs, dropping out of school before completing high school is a deficit that follows one throughout life and significantly limits one's future earnings, opportunities, and self-esteem. From a more pragmatic and cost-benefit perspective, for every student with whom a school counselor is successful in finding ways to keep him or her in school, the school obtains the amount of average state aid for that individual. Such an amount could range from a couple of thousand dollars annually to four or five thousand or more in a particular state and locality. Thus, in such situations, the measure of effective school counseling is not some abstract, private and positive result, it is actual dollars in the school's budget that derive from the school counselor's role in drop-out prevention.

School counselors also play many other roles about which school administrators should care. These roles are less directly related to student academic progress but are nevertheless important. For example, given the changing family structures in the United States–the disintegration of intact two parent families, the rise in the number of single parents, the inability of parents, because of economic necessity and job requirements, to be at home when their children leave for school or return home, the rise in child neglect or abuse–many schools have become child-rearing institutions. Schools are for many children the most secure and predictable institutions in their lives. They are sources of food for their bodies as well as for their minds. They are places where children and adolescents bring their despair, their loneliness, their pain. And, no amount of argument that these are not issues that schools should deal with will change the reality that these are the physical and psychological conditions that some students bring with them, that preoccupy them, and mediate their ability to fully participate in the academic and social life of the school. For many of these children the school counseling office is a haven of support and caring, of personal attention, that is rarely available in other aspects of their lives. Although teachers undoubtedly serve in such roles for some of these students, their schedules and academic obligations make it difficult to work with these types of student needs in a classroom context. Both by training and by opportunity, school counselors can provide the mentoring, the concern, the bridge between the school, the child and the family, the identification and brokering of resources needed by the child or adolescent to sustain a reason for remaining in school, to keep their hopes alive, to reduce their fears and anxieties so that students can devote their attention to academic roles.

School counselors frequently discharge their roles on a one-to-one or individual basis with students who are experiencing difficulties ranging from normal developmental problems to the more serious problems of psychological distress, substance abuse, violent behavior, academic failure, and premature school leaving. However, school counselors also employ many other techniques to work with students. These may include support groups for students experiencing similar types of concerns: living in a divorcing family, becoming part of a blended family, learning to manage anger or stress. Counselors may provide their own curriculum, within group guidance units, in academic classes, during or after school or in activity periods, that is intended to provide students information and skills related to conflict resolution, career planning and choice, study skills, preparing for college entrance, job search and interview processes, goal-setting, choosing among schools or curricula. They may use testing to help students broaden their horizons about their potential, to clarify their strengths and interests, to identify behaviors they can modify or learn. School administrators should care about school counseling in these circumstances because it results in increased student motivation and wiser choices than would otherwise occur, as well as the normalizing of stress and anxiety for many students experiencing problems external to the school that have an impact on their academic work.

The seriousness of many of the problems that students experience in contemporary society–anger, violence, vandalism, extensive absenteeism, teenage pregnancy, substance abuse and dependency, AIDS, suicide–have continued to expand the problems that school counselors are expected to address and the ways by which school counselors are expected to function in relation to students, parents, and the community at large. Increasingly, in many of these matters, school counselors are expected to serve as a part of teams, sometimes labeled as Instructional Support Teams or Student Assistance Programs, that bring all of the resources of the school and the community to bear on the needs of particular students. In such cases, depending upon the form and severity of a student's problem, the school counselor may be involved with early identification of the problem, coordination with teachers about the behavioral manifestations of the problem in the classroom, or may liaison with other specialists in the school and in the community–school psychologists, social workers, community mental health workers, psychiatrists–to determine what interventions or what other community resources might be employed to deal with the problem. In some such cases, counselors coordinate and/or monitor the functioning and results of these teams.

Beyond the matter of teams within the school to deal with at risk students, there is also a growing trend, particularly in the inner city, to use the school as the centerpiece for integrated services–counseling, medical, financial, etc.–that bring to bear available community resources in one place for families that are in different types of dysfunction or distress. In these cases, again, the school counselor is involved either as a referral agent for families in need of a program of intervention or in providing counseling to the children of these families and to the parents themselves.

What has not been discussed here are other roles that school counselors can play that are in support of the administrator or the classroom teacher. Certainly, one of these is as a resource person. The counselor can provide feedback to administrators about the outcomes students are experiencing as they leave school to start work or to begin postsecondary education or other options. Often, follow-up studies of students by counselors can identify emerging trends in opportunities or changes in skill requirements that schools can anticipate and then address. School counselors in their contacts with mental health professionals, employers, law enforcement and family court representatives in the community can serve as a resource to administrators about how best to use these resources and for what purposes. In their communications with parents, school counselors serve as visible interpreters of school policies and school opportunities and they obtain feedback from parents about how the school can communicate more effectively or provide particular opportunities for students. In support of teachers, counselors can serve as a referral source for students who are having particular difficulty in a specific classroom or who are otherwise functioning inappropriately or inadequately. Frequently, school counselors serve as confidential resources to teachers as they express their personal frustration and stress and seek the opportunity to put it into perspective. Counselors also serve teachers in talking with them about the needs of particular students to be included in specific types of support groups, for staffing or case conferences about behavioral management, for referral beyond the school, and they often engage as a moderator and facilitator in parental conferences with teachers. Many of these activities are important elements contributing to the mental wellness of the school climate and to the quality of communication within the school and between the school and community.

While there are many other reasons why school administrators should care about school counseling, those cited above represent some of the major factors. Other reasons are expressed in the chapters that follow. Clearly, one of the challenges for school administrators in the twenty-first century will be the need to use all of the assets available to improve the school's meaningfulness to students as both a nurturing and intellectually challenging opportunity for them and as a place through which they can navigate in purposeful and productive ways. A key asset in meeting these goals is school counseling–a process and a profession about which school administrators should care.

References

...or Association. (1996). Role statement, *...ide, 1996-97* (pp. 21-23). Alexandria,

...elors Association. (1996). Ethical *...ervices Guide, 1996-97.* (pp. 44-51). ...thor.

...lationship of counselors to school *...idance and Counseling in the Nation's ...ers.* Washington, DC. The American ...ssociation.

...., Ed.D., is Distinguished Professor of Education and Associate Dean for Graduate Programs, Research, and Technology, The College of Education, The Pennsylvania State University, University Park, Penn.

Chapter 1

What a School Administrator Needs to Know About *Comprehensive School Counseling Programs*

Zark VanZandt, Karen H. Burke, & Michael J. DeRespino

Administrators who understand the comprehensive developmental guidance and counseling model not only position themselves to improve programs and services to students and the community, but they also enhance their ability to provide effective administrative leadership for guidance and counseling programs. This capsule explains the comprehensive developmental model and offers suggestions for how administrators can be more actively engaged in the development, implementation, and evaluation of quality guidance and counseling programs.

What is a Comprehensive Developmental School Counseling Program?

A comprehensive developmental school counseling program is the combination of "developmental guidance" and "counseling." Schmidt (1993) defined developmental guidance as a sequential program of school-wide "activities and services designed to help students focus on the attainment of knowledge and skills for developing healthy life goals and acquiring the behaviors to reach those goals"; whereas counseling relationships are defined as "ongoing helping processes, confidential in nature, that assist people in focusing on personal concerns, planning strategies to address specific issues, and evaluating their success in carrying out these plans" (p. 34).

According to Gysbers (1990), the purpose of the comprehensive developmental model is to assure that guidance program efforts reach all students, that guidance is viewed as a program with specific content rather than as an ancillary service, that program accountability is achieved, and that certain competencies are attained as a result of guidance program efforts. There are several benefits to this comprehensive model:

- the program is aligned with national models of excellence
- there are more opportunities for collaboration with teachers, parents, and the community
- students make better use of the school counseling program
- roles are more clearly defined
- the framework fosters more valid program evaluation

Why Administrators are Key to the Program's Success

School administrators are school leaders. A good administrator has a visionary sense of where the school district is headed and how all the school programs complement each other in moving toward this vision. School counselors need to meet regularly with administrators to share in this vision and to discuss how the school counseling program can link critical K-12 programs and services that meet students' needs and support the school system's vision and mission.

Certainly, school programs can survive without an administrator's involvement, but rarely do they thrive. A significant observation from the pilot sites for the *Get a Life* Personal Planning Portfolio (VanZandt, 1994) was that administrative support and involvement was critical to the success of the portfolio project. When administrators were well-informed and participating in training, the rest of the staff took the project seriously and remained focused on its goals. However, passive support by administrators was reflected in schools where the portfolio was seen as an add-on more than as a complement to school restructuring and renewal.

Only school administrators and school counselors are directly responsible for attending to the needs of ALL students. As team players, they can create a systemic, interdependent approach to providing students with the best possible opportunities for learning and growing.

Theoretical Models

The Missouri Model (Gysbers, 1990) and Myrick's (1993) developmental approach provide theoretical frameworks for creating comprehensive developmental school counseling programs . The Missouri Model provides an organizational plan for program development, whereas the Myrick model offers a more philosophical and theoretical orientation.

The primary purpose of the Missouri Model is to provide a framework for the development, implementation, and evaluation of comprehensive and systematic guidance programs (Gysbers, 1990). The model has four major components:

> Guidance Curriculum (e.g., structured groups, classroom guidance units);
>
> Individual Planning (e.g., advising, assessment, placement and follow-up);
>
> Responsive Services (e.g., individual and group counseling, consultation, and referral); and System Support (e.g., management, coordination, community outreach, and public relations).

According to Myrick (1993), the developmental approach considers the nature of human development, including general stages and tasks that most individuals experience as they mature from childhood to adulthood, centers on developing positive self-concepts, and acknowledges that one's self-concept is formed and reformed through experience and education. Developmental guidance and counseling assumes that human nature moves individuals sequentially and positively toward self-enhancement and self-worth, but that this innate drive for personal expression and uniqueness often is affected by environmental forces. Myrick suggests practical methods for delivering the comprehensive development program through collaborative efforts like Teacher-Advisor Programs, Peer Facilitator projects, large group guidance activities, and case consultation models.

School districts may borrow from these or other national models to create their own individualized program plans. Attention to local needs, existing resources, and management preferences will suggest how the models may be adapted and refined to complement the district's mission.

Practical Management Issues

School administrators can provide valuable expertise in addressing the management issues that often provide major challenges for school counseling programs. These issues include (a) program leadership, (b) supervision, (c) the written plan, (d) scope and sequence guidance curriculum, (e) staffing, (f) school counseling advisory committees, and (g) program accountability.

Program Leadership

Just as an academic department requires the leadership of a chairperson, the school counseling program also requires strong leadership. In comprehensive developmental programs, the program coordinator should have K–12 responsibilities. The archaic model of making a high school counselor the director or coordinator does not reflect current school administration paradigms. The person who is most respected and who can most effectively shape a systemic model of excellence should be tapped for this leadership role.

Supervision

School counselors need two kinds of supervision: administrative and clinical. School administrators can certainly assist with the administrative supervision, especially in assessing how counselors are accountable to their program mission and goals. However, school counselors, because of the specialized nature of their profession, possess professional counseling skills that can only be supervised by highly qualified counselors. Some schools contract for doctoral-level supervision, while some schools create peer supervision models to address this need. Administrators can provide essential assistance by understanding the need for clinical supervision and by providing the logistical support to operationalize a supervision plan.

The Written Plan

Many states now require school counseling programs to have a written comprehensive program plan. Insist that counselors in your district develop a plan that is a working document "dynamically responsive to the changing needs of students and society" (Bleuer, 1990, p. 2), not one that just sits on a shelf. Create a process whereby all counselors are involved in and invested in the development as well as the implementation of the plan (VanZandt & Hayslip, 1994). Ensure that the school counseling plan and program are linked to the district's mission statement and the state's mandates and initiatives.

Scope and Sequence Guidance Curriculum

The heart of the school counseling program should be its curriculum (Buchan & VanZandt, 1997). If counselors at all levels are not involved in the guidance curriculum, developing an Action Plan to create a curriculum that is coordinated, sequential and focused on the developmental needs of students is a critical component. Help counselors and classroom teachers create an integrated curriculum that links academic, career, and social-personal lessons as an integral part of the school's curriculum. If counselors lack the skills to create a comprehensive guidance curriculum, provide professional development opportunities that focus on their skill needs.

Staffing

An effective comprehensive guidance program must include a sufficient number of staff members who are knowledgeable, capable, and who possess a strong sense of self-worth. Develop a rubric consisting of specific criteria that counselors should possess for the various roles within the district. Use the rubric to hire staff who are committed to building assets in students and staff. Encourage staff to focus on prevention instead of remediation. Support funding for ongoing training tailored to the needs of the counselors. Provide administrative supervision which encourages and nurtures professional growth. Assist and support mentorships.

School Counseling Advisory Committees

Overseeing the comprehensive developmental counseling program cannot be left to chance or to one individual. Facilitate the organization of an advisory committee that is comprised of a small, representative group which includes a well-respected K–12 administrator. The focus of this advisory committee should be to guide the implementation of the program. Help schedule regular meetings that have advance agendas which include reviewing, discussing, and evaluating program priorities. Encourage the advisory committee to promote high standards and high expectations by providing a strong commitment to the goals established.

Program Accountability

Assist counselors in articulating specific criteria to measure the effectiveness of the comprehensive program. Help counselors identify the kind of "meaningful information" they should be collecting to demonstrate their responsiveness to student needs and their commitment and dedication to program goals and objectives. Help the counselors share such information on a regular basis with the school board, staff, parents, students, and members of the community.

Conclusion

A strong collaborative relationship between school administrators and school counselors can eliminate old paradigms of delivery and can foster innovative approaches that have a tremendous impact on students' lives. Creating such systemic change requires vision, commitment, understanding, risk-taking, dynamic leadership... and patience.

References

Bleuer, J. (1990). Comprehensive guidance program design. *ERIC/CAPS Digests: Covering critical issues and topics in guidance, counseling, and human services.* Ann Arbor, MI: ERIC/CAPS.

Buchan, B.A., & VanZandt, Z. (1997). *Lessons for life: A career development curriculum for busy educators.* Englewood Cliffs, NJ: Prentice Hall Direct.

Gysbers, N. C. (Ed.). (1990). *Comprehensive guidance programs that work.* Ann Arbor, MI: ERIC/CAPS Clearinghouse.

Myrick, R. D. (1993). *Developmental guidance and counseling: A practical approach* (2nd ed.). Minneapolis: Educational Media.

Schmidt, J. J. (1993). *Counseling in schools: Essential services and comprehensive programs.* Boston: Allyn & Bacon.

VanZandt, C. E. (1994, March). *Get a Life: Your personal planning portfolio for career development.* Pilot Site Summary Report. Washington, DC: National Occupational Information Coordinating Committee.

VanZandt, C. E., & Hayslip, J. B. (1994). *Your comprehensive school guidance and counseling program: A handbook of practical activities.* New York: Longman.

Zark VanZandt, Ed. D., is Professor and Chair, Counselor Education Program, Department of Human Resource Development, University of Southern Maine, Gorham, ME.

Karen H. Burke is Director of Curriculum, M.S.A.D. #6, Bar Mills, ME.

Michael J. DeRespino, is a graduate assistant and school counseling student, Counselor Education Program, University of Southern Maine, Gorham, ME.

Chapter 2

What a School Administrator Needs to Know About the Elementary School Counseling Curriculum

Sherry Clayton Baldwin, Kathleen K. Noyes, & Mary D. Deck

A school administrator needs to be well aware of both general principles and specific "best practices" that guide the elementary school guidance curriculum. The following capsule offers a framework for discussion and planning between administrator and counselor in developing a comprehensive, developmental school counseling plan which meets students' needs.

Principle One

The elementary school guidance curriculum is sequential, developmental, and comprehensive. There is a clear, written plan that outlines the age-appropriate curriculum offerings at each grade/developmental level.

Best Practices

The elementary guidance curriculum is integral to the total mission of the school and incorporates basic philosophical beliefs educators hold about how to foster student success. The guidance curriculum is an essential component of the complete educational experience of elementary students and, thus, is not an ancillary or "add-on" program.

The guidance curriculum is expected to be clearly aligned with any state or district curriculum mandates, individual school policies, and national initiatives such as those endorsed by the American School Counseling Association. A school counselor will be able to show in the comprehensive, developmental school counseling plan how these frameworks are included (Gysbers, 1990). There must be clear articulation of the rationale for the guidance curriculum to all school populations—from the local school management team to the Parent-Teacher Association. Administrator and counselor alike have a responsibility to promote, market, and build support for the guidance curriculum as a vital part of the comprehensive, developmental school counseling plan and of the total school plan.

The elementary school counselor is always mindful of the developmental needs of children in grades kindergarten through fifth (Paisley & Hubbard, 1994). With a knowledge of the physical, cognitive, and social and emotional growth patterns of elementary children, the school counselor develops a list of topics for the guidance curriculum that reflects these developmental needs. Common topics might include: safety, social skills, career awareness, character ethics, and friendships skills (Baker, 1992; Myrick, 1993). After the developmental topics are determined, the guidance curriculum plan can focus on the scope and sequence of the topics/lessons at each grade level and the yearly plan for the presentation of each activity.

Lesson activities and the length of lessons vary with the ages and developmental levels of the students. Whereas a fifth grade class might work on a weekly lesson for a forty-five minute period, a kindergarten lesson might be ten minutes, twice a week. Scheduling the lessons must be driven by developmental needs and appropriate educational rationales rather than any arbitrary scheduling vehicle. School administrators need to pay attention to the message that is conveyed by the delivery of the guidance curriculum.

The guidance curriculum is delivered by all school personnel, not just the school counselor. Perhaps a building custodian mentors a fifth grade student in how recycled paper is prepared for pick-up. A classroom teacher may incorporate a lesson on using mediation in a social studies class. The cafeteria staff may use a "helpers" bulletin board to encourage students to self-monitor during lunch periods. Everyone in the school participates in the implementation of the guidance curriculum.

Principle Two

The elementary guidance curriculum is designed to be proactive, preventative, and is offered to ALL children in the school. The very nature of curricula underscores the belief that by providing age-appropriate activities focusing on basic educational and emotional needs that all students can realize healthy benefits.

Best Practices

In order to minimize the "crisis" or "problem-oriented" focus present in some school counseling programs, the guidance curriculum must be seen as a valuable activity that is rarely canceled, interrupted, or dropped at various times of the year (such as during state/district testing programs). Counselors who are "pulled out" of a classroom guidance lesson to handle a crisis send a powerful, negative message to faculty and students about the importance of the guidance activity. Counselors who are forced to abandon all classroom guidance lessons for weeks to conduct or oversee testing programs seriously damage the preventative, sequential, and developmental underpinnings of an appropriate school counseling program.

The elementary school counselor will be able to show an administrator the links between what is planned for the guidance curriculum and the counseling theories that promote a proactive, preventative approach. For example, a school counselor might be developing classroom guidance lessons based on William Glasser's (1992) Choice Theory and will be able to link that theoretical base to the content of the lesson on the five basic needs all people have (safety, love and belonging, power, fun, and freedom).

The proactive, preventative, and inclusive guidance curriculum will be known and supported by all school personnel. If the stated goal of the guidance curriculum is "TO HELP STUDENTS BE PRODUCTIVE AND SUCCESSFUL AT SCHOOL," the administrator will model and endorse policies that foster this goal.

Principle Three

School counselors model educational strategies and techniques in the implementation of the guidance curriculum. The counselor will be proficient in employing effective practices in areas such as facilitating classroom guidance, maintaining classroom discipline, consulting with staff, and managing and evaluating the implementation of the guidance curriculum.

Best Practices

In schools where instructional activities such as Cooperative Learning, Paideia Seminars, mediation, skillstreaming, and Junior Great Books are used, the school counselor demonstrates the ability to integrate these methods into the delivery of the guidance curriculum.

The school counselor looks for creative ways to integrate guidance curriculum with other curriculum areas and to emphasize school-wide efforts, such as character education. School-wide management policies should be in place in the delivery of the guidance curriculum also. For example, if a school is using a lead-management program, it is appropriate to expect the school counselor to model this approach when planning, promoting, and delivering the guidance curriculum (Glasser, 1992).

Evaluation and review are crucial elements in maintaining a quality guidance curriculum. Needs assessments provide input into the guidance curriculum planning process as the written, yearly plan is developed and implemented (Gysbers & Henderson, 1994). Administrators and counselors review this plan annually and determine what changes are needed.

Conclusion

These principles and "best practices" indicate the collaboration required between administrators and school counselors in the development and implementation of a vital, flourishing elementary school guidance curriculum as part of the total elementary school counseling program. Administrators and school counselors have different roles, but it is essential that they are united in their understanding and support of the purpose and goals of the elementary school counseling curriculum.

References

Baker, S. B. (1992). *School counseling for the twenty-first century.* New York, NY: Macmillan Publishing.

Glasser, W. (1992). *The quality school.* New York, NY: Harper Collins.

Gysbers, N. C. (1990). *Comprehensive guidance programs that work.* Ann Arbor, MI: ERIC/CAPS Clearinghouse.

Gysbers, N. C., & Henderson, P. (1994). *Developing and managing your school guidance program.* Alexandria, VA: American Counseling Association.

Myrick, R. D. (1993). *Developmental guidance counseling: A practical approach.* Minneapolis, MN: Educational Media Corporation.

Paisley, P. O., & Hubbard, G. T. (1994). *Developmental school counseling programs: From theory to practice.* Alexandria, VA: American Counseling Association.

Sherry Clayton Baldwin, Ph.D., is a school counselor in the Buncombe County Schools in Asheville, NC and is an affiliate graduate faculty member in Counselor Education at Western Carolina University, Cullowhee, NC.

Kathleen K. Noyes, Ed.S., is an elementary school principal at Haw Creek Elementary School in Asheville, NC.

Mary D. Deck, Ph. D., is a counselor educator and School Counseling Program Leader at Western Carolina University, Cullowhee, NC.

Special thanks to Patricia A. Crawford, M. Ed., elementary school counselor at Brevard Elementary School, Brevard, NC, Transylvania County Schools for her suggestions and input.

Chapter 3

What a School Administrator Needs to Know About the School Counselor's Curriculum at the Secondary School Level

Gary E. Goodnough and James R. Dick

The school counselor's curriculum is an integral part of a comprehensive developmental guidance and counseling program at the secondary level. Such programs have been recommended "good practice" within the school counseling profession since the early 1980s (Myrick, 1993). A major thrust towards comprehensive developmental programs emerged from the tendency of "traditional" counselors to spend too much time with students at either end of the continuum of student performance. In this outdated model, counselors' time was consumed by very troubled students, on the one hand, and very able, college-bound students, on the other. Left out were the vast majority of students in the middle. Comprehensive developmental programs rectify this inequality of student access to counselors through an approach that systematically addresses the developmental needs of *all* students.

Within the comprehensive approach, student needs are addressed through four programmatic strands: individual planning, responsive services, systems support, and curriculum. Planning can take the form of a four-year academic and career plan with each incoming ninth grade student and her family. This plan can be revised and updated on a continual basis. In counseling and responsive services, counselors respond to the various needs that arise. Often this involves a program of group and individual counseling; consulting with administrators, teachers, and parents; and maintaining and utilizing a list of referral services. In order to effectively implement a developmental approach, counselors need to recognize limitations on their time and therapeutic abilities. Thus, it is important for them to widely refer (and follow up) to other professionals and community agencies. In the third programmatic strand, counselors work to support the guidance program through professional development, research, and preparation. Finally, a curriculum of guidance and counseling competencies is implemented systematically throughout the secondary school years. (Gysbers & Henderson, 1994).

Formulating the Guidance and Counseling Curriculum

As it is a major strand of developmental programs in secondary schools, a carefully planned, comprehensive curriculum is of vital import. Its formulation should be systematic and thorough and should include assessing the needs of students and other stakeholders, such as teachers, parents, and business people. These needs relate to students' educational, career, social, and personal development. After needs are assessed, the information is translated into competencies that students are expected to attain at different grade levels. A curriculum is then written that details how the competencies can be met and who within the school will assume responsibility for ensuring their completion. Typically, school administrators and counselors assume strong leadership roles in organizing and coordinating the implementation of the curriculum.

Student Competencies in the Guidance Curriculum

It is important that student competencies in the guidance curriculum be locally determined. Nevertheless, some states have created a series of competencies that localities can look to when creating their own programs. For instance, The New Hampshire Comprehensive Guidance Program (Carr, Brook, Hayslip, Williams, & Zwolinski, 1997) organizes competencies within broad areas. The largest area is self-understanding. Within this competency area, units are developed which help high school students demonstrate an understanding of their attitudes, values, abilities, aptitudes, interests, and feelings. A second major area of competency deals with helping students attain a higher level of global and social understanding. This includes teaching students interpersonal communication skills, and social and personal responsibility. A third vital curriculum area involves teaching students decision-making skills, including how to set goals, identify problems, gather and analyze information, explore options, and initiate action. These three competency areas relate not only to self-development, but also to development in connection with academics and preparation for initial career decision-making.

The guidance curriculum directly supports the teaching of critical thinking skills by motivating students to take an active role in learning through processing information, drawing conclusions, and recognizing implications of decisions. Additional competencies include providing students with a structured learning environment wherein they demonstrate that they understand the relationship between achieving academically and their future career training. The school-to-work connection evident in the curriculum thus far is expanded upon in the final group of competencies.

Given the necessity of actively fostering the school-to-work connection, the secondary guidance curriculum provides a formal structure for students to understand how self-concept relates to career choice (e.g., "If I fail a class, I am not a failure"). Further, the curriculum focuses on teaching students *how* to prepare for various careers. Additional competencies center around economic issues of personal budgeting and marketability of self. Finally, the New Hampshire guidance curriculum organizes and provides competencies for teaching students to understand the world of work. This includes knowing the characteristics of careers that interest them, work behaviors and habits expected by employers, and the structure of the workplace and how it functions (Carr et al., 1997).

Taken together and organized sequentially, the above

competencies provide an example of a blueprint for a secondary guidance and counseling curriculum. A legitimate and important question remains: How is the curriculum organized and integrated into a high school schedule?

Curriculum Implementation

Although the title of this capsule is "the school counselor's curriculum at the secondary school level," it is important that the sole responsibility for the curriculum and its implementation *not* be the school counselor's. A comprehensive school counseling program, of which the curriculum is a central component, is a school-wide endeavor and, as such, is the responsibility of the entire school community under the leadership of building administrators. As a building-wide program, there are three common ways that the curriculum is implemented. Although we will describe each separately, usually all three methods are used in schools.

In the first method, teachers infuse the guidance curriculum into their already existing subject areas. For example, English and Language Arts teachers can foster students' self-understanding by brainstorming attitudes, values, and interests towards work. Subsequently, students can use what they have brainstormed to write an essay on their current beliefs and how these beliefs relate to students' future plans (Rogala, Lambert, & Verhage, 1991). In history class, teachers and students can discuss the career development paths of a number of famous individuals. This discussion can serve as a springboard for examining students' own career development issues. Infusing the guidance curriculum this way, teachers use the content of the guidance curriculum and combine it with the objectives they are teaching (e.g., essay writing or history) to provide students an integrated curriculum.

The second delivery modality is based upon counselor and teacher collaboration. It is similar to the first modality in that it occurs in the traditional classroom setting and the activities meet the curriculum goals of both the subject area and the guidance curriculum. However, in contrast to the first delivery modality, here counselors *join* with teachers and work together. For instance, twelfth grade English teachers and school counselors

18

may collaborate to create a comprehensive career unit that incorporates competencies– from writing cover letters and resumes to preparing for and experiencing mock interviews with community members.

Another way to deliver the guidance curriculum is by counselors themselves teaching large and small groups of students. For example, counselors administer interest inventories to sophomores and then provide a group interpretation (allowing, of course, for individual appointments as needed or requested by students and parents). Also, they frequently provide interpersonal, educational, and career information to groups of students both in a planned, sequential manner as well as in a timely fashion as it becomes available. Particularly when counselors are the direct providers of the curriculum, they need the full and explicit support of teachers and administrators. Regardless of who delivers the guidance curriculum, it is crucial that it not be viewed as an ancillary service, but as a program central to the mission of the school.

Conclusion

The outcomes associated with a fully implemented and successful guidance curriculum are numerous and their necessity well-documented. The changing nature of society and the workforce calls for school programs to prepare students to be developmentally ready to transition successfully to postsecondary education and the world of work. This developmental readiness does not just happen for many students. It is the secondary school's responsibility to systematically implement a curriculum geared toward ensuring that students understand themselves as developing individuals who comprehend the nature of the workplace, who can think critically, and who can make decisions in their best interest. The guidance curriculum at the secondary level is the glue that connects these important components for educating students to lead healthy lives as individuals, family members, contributing citizens, and satisfied workers.

References

Carr, J. V., Brook, C. A., Hayslip, J. B., Williams, F., & Zwolinski, M. (1997). *A manual for a comprehensive career guidance and counseling program.* Concord, NH: New Hampshire Comprehensive Guidance and Counseling Program, Inc.

Gyspers, N. C., & Henderson, P. (1994). *Developing and managing your school guidance program.* Alexandria, VA: American Counseling Association.

Myrick, R. D. (1993). *Developmental guidance and counseling: A practical approach.* Minneapolis, MN: Educational Media Corporation.

Rogala, J. A., Lambert, R., & Verhage K. (Eds.). (1991). *Developmental classroom activities for use with national career development guidelines.* Madison, WI: University System Board of Regents.

Gary E. Goodnough, Ph.D., NCC, is Assistant Professor, Department of Education, Plymouth State College, Plymouth NH.

James R. Dick, M.Ed., is Assistant Superintendent, Ligonier School District, Ligonier, PA.

Chapter 4

What a School Administrator
Needs To Know About
National Standards for
School Counseling Programs

Carol A. Dahir

Counseling Is Important in School

Research has demonstrated (Borders & Drury, 1992) that school counseling is an integral component of the programs and services that can best serve student needs. School counselors are a significant positive force in the lives of children and in the school environment (Greer & Richardson, 1992). Boyer (1988), in his description of the role of the school counselor stated:

> Today, in most high schools, counselors are not only expected to advise students about college, they are also asked to police for drugs, keep records of dropouts, reduce teenage pregnancy, check traffic in the halls, smooth out the tempers of irate parents, and give aid and comfort to battered and neglected children. School counselors are expected to do what our communities, our homes and our churches have not been able to accomplish, and if they cannot, we condemn them for failing to fulfill our high-minded expectations (p. 3).

School counselors coordinate the objectives, strategies, and activities of a comprehensive and developmental school counseling program to meet the personal, social, educational and career development needs of all students. School counselors help students strive to meet the challenges and demands of the school system and prepare for life after high school. School counselors call attention to situations in schools that are defeating or frustrating students and thereby hindering their success.

Why do We Need National Standards for School Counseling Programs?

The American School Counselor Association's (ASCA) decision to develop national standards for school counseling programs provides an opportunity for the school counseling community to implement the goals deemed important by the profession and to promote ASCA's mission to ensure student success in school. National standards for school counseling programs are what ASCA believes to be the essential elements of a quality school counseling program. They are intended to guide states, districts, and individual schools in developing, planning, implementing and evaluating a school counseling program that is comprehensive, developmental, and systematic. The standards address program content and the learning opportunities (competencies) that all students should experience as a result of participating in a school counseling program.

The *National Standards for School Counseling Programs* focuses on what all students, from pre-kindergarten through grade twelve, should know, understand, and be able to do as a result of participating in a school counseling program. The standards blend theory and practice and are based upon the three widely accepted and interrelated areas that comprise school counseling programs:

(a) academic development,
(b) career development, and
(c) personal and social development.

What Will National Standards Accomplish for Your School System?

National standards for school counseling programs will
1. Establish the school counseling program as an integral

component of the academic mission of your school.
2. Ensure equitable access to school counseling services for all students provided by a credentialed school counselor.
3. Identify the knowledge and skills that all students should acquire as a result of the K–12 school counseling program.
4. Ensure that your school counseling program is comprehensive in design and delivered in a systematic fashion to all students.

National standards for school counseling programs promote and enhance the learning process. School counseling programs contribute the essential personal, social, educational, and career development support for students to overcome obstacles to school achievement and to ensure access to appropriate services for students with varying individual needs (Wurtz, 1995).

How Were the National Standards Developed?

The development of national standards for school counseling programs required an examination of theory, research, and practice to ensure that all aspects of school counseling are considered. The process solicited a broad-based involvement from school counselors.

In September of 1995, a revised seventy-seven item survey instrument was mailed to 2000 ASCA members who were employed either as a school counselor or as a counselor supervisor. The respondents provided essential information as to
(a) school counselor attitudes toward developing national standards for school counseling programs;
(b) the purpose that standards would serve; and
(c) what content areas would be included in the standards for school counseling programs.

A statistically sound and sufficiently comprehensive data analysis was required to support the foundation for standards development. The publishers of the ACT (American College Test) served as research consultants and coordinators for the collection of information. Furthermore, they donated the personnel and resources necessary to ensure that the survey's design, distribution, and analysis followed accepted research practices.

The results of the survey revealed that school counselors

1. Strongly and broadly supported the development of national standards.
2. Demonstrated that program priorities should be based upon student developmental needs.
3. Supported an increased emphasis in personal/social, academic, and career development activities.
4. Advocated for system support activities that are directly connected to supporting or assisting students needs.

How Do We Implement the National Standards?

The National Standards for School Counseling Programs is the most contemporary and cutting edge vision of a quality school counseling program. It represents the skills, strategies and applications that school counselors believe should be acquired by all students as a result of participating in school counseling programs.

Making the shift to a standards-based school counseling program requires the commitment of school counselors to accept the ownership of standards. This can mean rethinking every aspect of a school counseling program: from the assessment of delivery methods and allocation of resources, to ensuring that all students have equitable access to services. Implementing a standards-based program requires school counselors to be willing to assume responsibility for the delivery of a quality program and to be accountable for student outcomes.

How do you begin to undertake this shift in thinking and in doing? The progression from the "what is" to the "what is to be" proceeds through several stages of development. These stages include Discussion, Planning, Program Design, Implementation, and Evaluation.

Discussion

The initial discussion about standards requires an awareness of what your program currently looks like and what it accomplishes. You need to use student data to examine student needs and how those needs relate to the mission of your school. It is important to consider questions such as

1. Why move to a standards-based school counseling program?
2. What will this change accomplish that is different from existing program outcomes?
3. Who will benefit?

Planning

Planning is essential to ensure you will accomplish what you set out to accomplish. Key planning questions include

1. What skills do your students need to acquire to make successful transitions to (a) each new level (e.g., elementary school to middle school), and (b) life after high school?
2. How does your current program compare with a standards-based program?
3. Where are the gaps?
4. What does your school and your community envision as important for your students?
5. Do you have an advisory committee in place that involves teachers, parents, students, and members of the community?

Program Design

The key program design questions are as follows:

1. What format makes the most sense for presenting your standards-based program?
2. Do you begin with goals and then develop student outcomes?
3. What language is your system using in their other educational reform undertakings?
4. Are your student expectations clear and focused?
5. Are the expectations measurable as indicators of performance or achievement?
6. Do your goals evolve from your mission statement and

your vision for your students?
7. How is the faculty involved?

Please note that school counseling standards must be written in a context that makes sense with your curriculum standards.

Implementation

A phase-in plan for the short-term and the long-term goals will help you establish benchmarks to help you monitor progress. Important implementation questions include:
1. Are the resources in place to begin the implementation?
2. Is the essential staff development in place for all involved in the program delivery (i.e., school counselors, other student service personnel, administrators, and faculty)?
3. Who will do what and when?
4. Have you communicated your vision and goals to parents and to your community?
5. Does your time-line make sense?
6. Is your program for all students?

Evaluation

Evaluation lays the groundwork for determining if you have achieved your goals and provides opportunities to assess at what level or to what degree students have acquired the skills you set out to impart. The information gained from the evaluation process tells you what students have learned and how your standards-based program has made a difference. This insight also tells you which accomplishments should be celebrated, what obstacles have been encountered, what mistakes have been made, and what challenges remain.

Making the transition to a standards-based school counseling program cannot happen overnight. Each school system faces challenges that are unique to its community. State initiatives may impact upon local implementation. The assessment of existing programs, services and practices is a thoughtful and lengthy process. Consensus among all the stakeholders takes time. You may be facing a development and implementation process that could take two to three years before you see results.

Standards provide the foundation to ensure equitable access to school counseling programs for *all* students. Standards will also raise the level of expectation for student outcomes and thus make excellence in school counseling possible. If you see standards as an opportunity to change the expectations and perceptions about your current school counseling program and to provide opportunities to enable all students to achieve success in school, then, let the conversation begin.

Additional information about *The National Standards for School Counseling Programs* can be obtained from:

The American School Counselor Association
801 North Fairfax Street, Suite 310
Alexandria, Virginia 22314
(703/683-2711).

References

American School Counselor Association. (1997). *The National Standards for School Counseling Programs.* Alexandria, VA.: Author.

Borders, D. L., & Drury, R. D. (1992). Comprehensive school counseling programs: A review for policy makers and practitioners. *Journal of Counseling and Development, 70,* 487-498.

Boyer, E. L. (1988). Exploring the future: Seeking new challenges. *Journal of College Admissions, 118,* 2 -8.

Greer, R., & Richardson, M. (1992). Restructuring the guidance delivery system: Implications for high school counselors. *School Counselor, 40,* 93-102.

Mitchell, R. (1996). *Front end alignment.* Washington, DC Education Trust.

Wurtz, E. (1995). National Education Goals Panel phone conversation. Washington, DC

Carol A. Dahir, Ed.D., is the Pupil Personnel Services Administrator at Nassau BOCES (Westbury, NY), ASCA National Standards and Research Chair, and an adjunct instructor at Hofstra University.

Chapter 5

What a School Administrator Needs to Know About the School Counselor's Role With Discipline

J. Ron Nelson, Rob McGregor, and Denise Robertson

Disruptive forms of behavior increasingly characterize students in our schools. The National School Safety Center has reported that students and school staff alike do not feel completely safe in schools (Stephens, 1995). The 26th annual Phi Delta Kappan Gallup Poll of the public's attitudes toward the public schools mirrors the concerns of educators about the safety of schools and the rates of disruptive behavior occurring in our schools (Elam, Rose, & Gallup, 1994). Addressing the increasing levels of disruptive behavior in schools is critical because well-developed antisocial behavior has been shown to lead to poor academic-, vocational-, and life-outcomes (e.g., Patterson, Reid, & Dishion, 1992). A comprehensive multilevel discipline program is necessary if schools are to respond effectively to the fundamental social changes that are occurring in our society and that are increasingly reflected in students' school behavior. Given their specialized training, it is evident that school counselors must play a key role in developing and implementing pragmatic and sustainable intervention approaches that meet the educational needs of a wide range of students.

Conceptual Model for School
Discipline Programs

Research on disruptive behavior suggests that schoolwide discipline programs must view such behavior as a socialization problem rather than a sickness (Shamise, 1991). Approaching disruptive behavior as a sickness has led schools to rely on indirect intervention approaches (e.g., insight-based counseling therapies, self-esteem enhancement) which are not powerful enough to solve intractable disruptive behavior (Eysenck, 1994). There is some evidence however, that discipline programs that focus on socializing students who exhibit disruptive behavior patterns are effective (e.g., Nelson, 1996). The effectiveness of these programs supports the concept that the majority of students behave according to social norms because key socializing agents (e.g., teachers) took the trouble to teach the social norms in a consistent manner. Thus, the conceptual model for a comprehensive multilevel discipline program must emphasize direct interventions within and across all school settings and must rely on teaching students acceptable social norms. The conceptual model should also include intervention approaches that are preventative (i.e., ensure that disruptive behavior does not commence or become entrenched as a result of the practices of the school) and remedial (i.e., must change chronic disruptive behavior) in nature.

Figure 1 presents a conceptual model for a comprehensive multilevel discipline program that emphasizes direct prevention and remedial intervention approaches. It depicts the relationship among student type, intervention approach, and role of the school counselor. The model identifies three types of students, ordered on a continuum, who need increasingly powerful preventative and remedial interventions:

(a) typical students who are not at risk for problems;
(b) at-risk students who are at risk of developing or are exhibiting disruptive behavior patterns; and
(c) chronic students who exhibit life course disruptive behavior patterns.

The model also identifies the primary prevention and remedial intervention approaches associated with each type of student and the role (supportive or primary) that the school counselor should take in implementing each intervention approach. The intervention approaches that encompass all three of these prevention and remediation levels are needed to effectively meet the needs of all students. The intervention approaches must also be directly linked to and coordinated with each other to be maximally effective.

Figure 1: Conceptual model for school discipline programs

Student Type	Intervention Approach	Counselor Role
Typical	Universal Interventions (Preventative and Remedial) • Effective teaching practices • Effective classroom management • Schoolwide discipline plan • Instruction in skills for school (e.g., school survival skills) and life success (e.g., conflict resolution, anger management)	Supportive
At-Risk (Developing or exhibiting disruptive behavior patterns	Targeted Interventions (Preventative and Remedial) • Identification of at-risk children • Intensive direct instruction in skills for school and life success • Caregiver support and caregiver management training • Consultant-based, 1-to-1 interventions • Mentor programs • Intensive academic interventions (if applicable)	Primary
Chronic (Exhibit life course disruptive behavior patterns)	Intensive Wraparound Interventions (Remedial) • Connection of children and caregivers to community-based social service agencies • Individually-tailored wraparound interventions (caregiver involvement in planning and treatment activities) • Coordination of school services with social service agencies • Referral to alternative placements, such as day-treatment centers, residential programs	Primary

Universal Interventions

Universal interventions are implemented on a school-wide basis and are designed to prevent disruptive behavior from developing or becoming entrenched as a result of the practices of the school. The interventions are considered to be universal because all students are exposed in the same way at the same level. Universal intervention approaches offer schools the greatest potential for preventing and diverting students at risk for developing disruptive behavior patterns. Additionally, the universal interventions provide the foundation upon which the targeted and intensive wraparound intervention approaches are implemented.

Inspection of Figure 1 reveals that there are four primary universal intervention approaches. Because there is a well-documented link between academic skill deficits and disruptive behavior (Kazdin, 1987), using effective teaching and classroom management practices designed to maximize the academic success of students represents a key component of a schoolwide discipline program. Building upon effective teaching and classroom management practices, schools must develop schoolwide discipline plans designed to promote positive social behavior. The basic goal of these plans is to achieve a school environment in which there is predictability in the moment-to-moment interactions between school staff and students and where it is clear to the students which behaviors are acceptable and which behaviors are unacceptable. Finally, school staff must teach students skills for school (e.g., being prepared for class, asking for help) and life success (e.g., resolving conflicts, controlling anger, and solving social problems). These skills should be interwoven into the standard academic curriculum and should be reinforced throughout the school year by the entire school staff.

School counselors play several supportive but nevertheless critical roles in implementing the universal intervention approaches. First, school counselors need to be aware of effective teaching and classroom management practices as well as strategies (e.g., peer coaching) for providing teachers feedback on their teaching and classroom management skills. Second, school counselors must help school staff to see that the basic goal of the

32

school-wide discipline plan should be to achieve a predictable school environment. This is critical because school staff often develop discipline plans that are narrow and reactive in scope, relying on punishment and exclusion from the school setting. Third, school counselors must not only help school staff to understand the importance of teaching students skills for school and life success but also help them to understand how to effectively teach students these skills. Finally, school counselors need to help faculty to work as a team so that they are able to set and maintain clear expectations for students.

Targeted Interventions

Targeted interventions are aimed at students who are at risk of developing or are exhibiting disruptive behavior patterns. The interventions are considered targeted because they are individually designed for students who do not respond to the universal interventions. Targeted interventions differ from universal interventions in that they are more intense in nature. In other words, targeted interventions essentially focus and enhance the impact of the universal interventions.

Inspection of Figure 1 shows that there are six primary targeted intervention approaches. Identifying students who do not respond to the universal interventions is the first step in implementing targeted interventions. Targeted interventions may be referred to as "selected" interventions because students select themselves out for more intensive interventions by not responding to the universal interventions. At-risk students need intensive direct instruction of school and life skills because they are not responding to the school and life skills taught in the classroom and, in some cases, to the curriculum and teaching practices. These students also need to be taught more directly how to discriminate which behaviors to use and not use under a variety of social and educational contexts. This is important because in many instances the problem for at-risk students is not "knowing how do it," but "doing it when it is required." Finally, at-risk students and their caregivers typically need a range of individualized interventions. These interventions include

(a) developing support networks and management

training for the caregivers;
(b) behavioral contracting;
(c) counseling;
(d) mentoring; and
(e) academic tutoring.

School counselors play a primary role in implementing the targeted intervention approaches. School counselors should work closely with school staff to ensure that at-risk students are identified and then provided the intervention approaches that are needed by the student and their caregivers. The ability of the school to provide a range of intervention approaches will not only be dependent upon the knowledge and skill levels of the school staff but upon the extent to which school staff have developed innovative approaches such as mentoring programs. Thus, school counselors must work with the school staff to develop a range of intervention approaches designed to enhance the success of at-risk students. Again, developing a range of targeted interventions requires school counselors to help school staff see beyond more traditional reactive intervention approaches such as detentions and suspensions.

Intensive Wraparound Interventions

Intensive wraparound interventions are aimed at students who exhibit severe, intractable life-course-persistent disruptive behavior patterns. The intervention approaches at this level are designed to involve multiple aspects of the student's life. These intervention approaches are collaborative in nature, involving peers, teachers, social agency personnel, and caregivers. The intervention approaches should be based on comprehensive assessments of the problem and should also involve a range of concerned individuals who are committed to establishing a long-term system of care. At a minimum, intensive wraparound interventions should include the teacher, peers, and caregivers (Cumblad, Epstein, Keeney, Marty, & Soderlund, 1996).

School counselors play a primary role in the development of intensive wraparound interventions. This is not to say that school counselors are solely responsible for developing the individualized, comprehensive interventions. Rather, school counselors are responsible for coordinating and interfacing with key individuals in the student's life. Coordinating and interfacing with the key individuals in the student's life is necessary to maximize the effectiveness of the intensive wraparound interventions. Additionally, school counselors will need to work with a range of other social agencies to set up the organizational and coordinating structures necessary to deliver intensive wraparound interventions.

References

Cumblad, C., Epstein, M. H., Keeney, K., Marty, T., & Soderlund, J. (1996). Children and adolescents network: A community-based program to serve individuals with serious emotional disturbance. *Special Services in the Schools, 11,* 97-118.

Elam, S., Rose, L., & Gallup, A. (1994). The 26th annual Phi Delta Kappan Gallup Poll of the public's attitudes toward the public schools. *Phi Delta Kappan, 26,* 42-56.

Eysenck, H. (1994). The outcome problem in psychotherapy: What have we learned? *Behavior Research and Therapy, 22,* 477-495.

Kazdin, A. (1987). *Conduct disorders in childhood and adolescence.* Beverly Hills, CA:Sage.

Nelson, J. R. (1996). Designing schools to meet the needs of students who exhibit disruptive behavior. *Journal of Emotional and Behavioral Disorders, 4,* 147-161.

Patterson, G. R., Reid, J. B., & Dishion, T. (1992). *Antisocial boys.* Eugene, OR: Castalia.

Shamise, S. (1991). Antisocial adolescents: Our treatments do not work—Where do we go from here? *Canadian Journal of Psychiatry, 26,* 357-364.

Stephens, R. D. (1995). *Safe schools: A handbook for violence prevention.* Bloomington, IN: National Educational Services.

J. Ron Nelson is Associate Professor of Education at Arizona State University, Tempe, AZ.

Rob McGregor is a school counselor with the Ellensburg School District, Ellensburg, WA.

Denise Robertson is a school counselor with Educational Service District No. 101, Spokane, WA.

What a School Administrator Needs to Know About the School Counselor's Role as Mental Health Services Broker

Brooke B. Collison, Judith L. Osborne, & Bill Layton

Who Provides Services in the Schools?

The traditional model of social service delivery in schools has included a certified or licensed school counselor. The core components of school counseling models have remained essentially the same since the mid-1950s when the number of school counselors increased as a direct result of federal dollars invested in counselor preparation [NDEA Institutes]. In recent years, those models have been changing because of different social and economic forces. One major change is the increase in the number of persons who provide mental health and other social services to school-aged youth and their families. Where it once was typical for the school counselor to "do it all," it is now more common for students or their families to be served by a variety of professionals and by several agencies. Service delivery takes place both in the school and outside. Services may be integrated with school efforts in some places and be totally independent and unrelated in others. In the more desirable integrated arrangements, school counselors are important players in the coordination and delivery of multiple services. School counselors of the future will need to be the brokers for mental health and other services, as well as be primary service delivery agents.

In this capsule, we refer to "school counselors" as those persons licensed or certified as school counselors and employed in schools. We refer to all other mental health and human service providers as "external service providers" to indicate that, in some way even though they may be school district employees, contract agents, or are employed by public or private social service agencies, they are external to the school counselor group. The difference may be that they are not licensed members of the school's bargaining unit, or that they are not typically located at a specific school under the direct responsibility of a building administrator. Most commonly, the difference between school counselors and external service providers is that the external provider has primary allegiance to an organization other than the school.

In contemporary times, the social and cultural issues and concerns of youth and families have reached a level of complexity that makes it nearly impossible for a single expert to address all matters of any youth or family. Specialists abound who address mental health issues, drug and alcohol issues, family counseling issues, physical and sexual abuse issues, youth gangs, and any number of other societal concerns. The yellow pages in any community will list mental health professionals, who claim to possess a multitude of specialties. School counselors know that some professionals are better at certain areas of practice than others. The school, in its mission to provide high quality service to all youth and their families, needs to find ways that services and service providers can be selected for quality and expertise. Negotiating matches of the right service providers with youth or families is a broker role that we believe is appropriate for the school counselor.

Issues Related to Other Providers
Working in Schools

If persons other than licensed school counselors work in the schools, or if they work with school-aged children or their families in any kind of relationship that implies approval of or endorsement by the school, then there are a set of issues that must be addressed. In particular, we list the following:

> (a) the requirements of state and federal mandates about service providers;
> (b) the qualifications, license, and authority of the external provider;
> (c) procedures related to access and use of school records and matters of confidentiality;
> (d) evaluation of service providers; and
> (e) the ultimate responsibility and liability involved when persons other than licensed school employees provide services to youth and families.

State and federal regulations must be considered when schools provide mental health or other social services. The general principle is that if the law requires specific services or if the law calls for service providers with certain qualifications, then the school can not offer that service from a less well qualified individual. This is most relevant when individual educational plans (IEPs) are developed for students and specific services are included in the IEP. There may be several potential service providers in a community, and school personnel (e.g., school counselors) must be mindful of qualification equivalencies in selecting or recommending providers.

A certificate or license does not guarantee quality service. It does, however, indicate to the public that a provider has met a set of minimum qualifications required by a state or other agency. A licensed (or certified) person can be held accountable for the service they provide. Licensing provides a mechanism for the unhappy client (or school) to complain. School counselors know that there are many different kinds of licensed and certified persons who provide mental health and other social services. Unlicensed persons also provide mental health and other social services in many communities. Some persons who may not be licensed might have legal authority to work with youth in schools — for example, court officials or probation officers. Persons may advertise and present themselves as service providers – especially if the title is not regulated by law – without benefit of any certificate or license. An unhappy client has only the civil courts for redress of grievance, and, in our opinion, a school that utilizes or recommends an unlicensed and unauthorized service provider is vulnerable to civil suits.

Both state and federal laws define school records. State laws usually define who has access to student records. Schools, under provision of federal or state guidelines, should define procedures for collection, maintenance, dissemination, and access to student records. With an increase in the number of persons who work with students –either in or out of the school–attention must be given to expanded use of student records. School counselors are ideally positioned to assist in developing records policies—especially when use involves other mental health service providers. Operating under the concept that records are owned by the clients and that schools or other agencies that maintain records are merely custodians of those records, schools should assure that proper releases for access or use of school records are signed by appropriate persons and are on file with the records that will be used. This is especially important in those cases where several agencies come together for a staffing of a single client case.

Evaluation of services performed is central to the way that schools operate. Teachers are evaluated by principals or other building administrators; school counselors are evaluated by administrators responsible for their services. External service providers need to be evaluated — the question is, "Who is the evaluator?" Preparation programs for school counselors seldom include personnel supervision or evaluation courses, nor is personnel evaluation usually required in the job of a school counselor. School counselors may be in the best position, however, to observe the services provided to students and their families and can make a quality assessment of those services. Schools should assure that good provider system evaluation systems are in place before granting access to students. In personnel evaluation procedures, school counselors can advise building administrators — the persons who have responsibility for personnel performance evaluation.

Liability generally cannot be given away. When schools implicitly or explicitly endorse external service providers, they expose themselves to the risks inherent with the provider. Risk or exposure should not prohibit schools from using external providers; however, risk management techniques would dictate that arrangements with providers who are not school employees must be spelled out in clear contract language. When providers work with school children – especially when referred by the school or if the service is provided in the school–then the school retains legal responsibility. To protect their own interests, schools need to have clear contracts and agreements about the kinds of issues listed above.

School Counselor Role

School counselors perform a number of specific functions related to external service providers. Initially, identification of youth to be served and coordination of the services to be provided is appropriate school counselor activity. If the school operates with multi-disciplinary teams (MDTs) to serve student needs, then school counselor involvement in the MDT could range from participant to management—depending on how the MDT is structured in a school. An appropriate role for the school counselor in an MDT is as student advocate—one who works to assure that student rights are protected and that student interests are served.

When providers enter the school to work with students, it cannot be assumed that they understand the school climate and the way that schools function. School counselors can familiarize non-school personnel with school policy and procedure, school culture, and student-teacher relations so that the outcome of external provider services is more likely to be positive; otherwise, as external providers begin to work with students or families they may violate informal school norms and be unable to achieve desired outcomes.

School counselors are positioned to both supervise and give input to the evaluation of mental health or other social service providers. Services should be coordinated or integrated to be most effective. Counselors can also observe service providers and develop feedback mechanisms with the providers that will let them know if their therapies are consistent with school goals and student expectations. In a day and age when it is common for a single student to be in treatment with several service providers or several agencies, it is very probable that a student could receive suggestions from one provider that would contradict suggestions or outcomes desired by a teacher or another service provider. School counselors can coordinate services through their broker role.

To provide quality comprehensive services to students and families, school counselors should be linked to as many community resources as possible. We do not suggest that school counselors should function solely as referral agents, but we do want counselor referrals to be the best that they can be. This requires that counselors develop comprehensive resource and referral networks with provider agencies.

Finally, we want school counselors to be the primary advisors to building administrators on mental health issues and policies. From their position as the licensed school employee who has the welfare of all students in mind, counselors can identify issues that need to be addressed in early, preventative stages just as they can name chronic problems that are experienced by larger numbers of students. If the climate or culture in a school building is such that it inhibits student learning, counselors should be in a position to advise principals and to assist in developing strategies to respond. Treating individual students may not be effective or appropriate.

Counselors should see themselves as brokers of mental health services. Their job is to see that students have what they need. They should operate in a managing style to match student and family needs with the resources and services required to assure student learning and good student adjustment.

References

Hobbs, B. B., & Collison, B. B. (1995). School-community agency collaboration: Implications for the school counselor. *The School Counselor, 43,* 58-65.

Osborne, J. L., & Collison, B. B. (in press). School counselors and external service providers: Conflict or complement. *The School Counselor.*

U.S. Department of Education (1996, May). *Putting the pieces together: Comprehensive school-linked strategies for children and families.* Washington, DC: Author.

U. S. Department of Education & American Educational Research Association (1995, April). *School-linked comprehensive services for children and families: What we know and what we need to know.* Washington, DC: Authors.

Brooke B. Collison is Professor of Counselor Education at Oregon State University, Corvallis, OR.

Judith L. Osborne is Assistant Professor of Counselor Education at Oregon State University, Corvallis, OR.

Bill Layton is Assistant Principal, Talmadge Middle School, Independence, OR.

What a School Administrator Needs to Know About *How School Counselors can Support Teachers*

Charlotte M. Wilkinson-Speltz & Ed Forsythe

Administrators and counselors share a commitment to having school counselors function in ways that both (a) promote student development and (b) nurture a school climate conducive to psychological health for everyone in the school setting (Hatfield & Nelson, 1990). To promote student development, counselors work closely with teachers to plan and teach classroom developmental guidance sessions, conduct school activities, and appraise students. To contribute to a positive school atmosphere, counselors provide in-service training, locate resource information, share committee work, and regularly consult with teams and individual teachers.

As a *facilitator for teacher support groups* a counselor can impact student development and can foster a nurturing school climate at the same time. Teacher support groups can focus on a variety of concerns. For beginning teachers a peer support group which continues throughout the year provides an additional means of staff development for them. The following sections focus on the rationale for peer support groups for beginning teachers, developmental stages in beginning teacher groups, the importance of administrative leadership, and characteristics of successful groups.

Rationale for Support Groups for Beginning Teachers

The authors shared the successful experience of establishing a beginning teachers support group. Both were committed to the belief that a peer support group for beginning educators would foster personal and professional growth as it offset the initial anxiety of entering the teaching profession. Three years of evaluations validated this belief (Wilkinson, 1994).

Offering a specific group for beginning teachers gives them an opportunity to reflect about their teaching experiences in a confidential setting. As they share feelings in a trusting, supportive atmosphere and as they process experiences together, they develop their conceptions of their roles as educators. In the group, new teachers begin to put their responsibilities and concerns in perspective, and they respond to challenges to move to higher developmental levels as professionals educators (Sprinthall & Thies-Sprinthall, 1983).

Developmental Stages in Beginning Teacher Groups

Studies of counselor-led support groups for beginning teachers indicate that new teachers move through four developmental stages (Thies-Sprinthall & Gerler, 1990). In the beginning, novice teachers are very focused on egocentric concerns about specific information that they need to succeed, such as forms and policies. Feelings often range from apathy because they do not believe they have anything to offer the group, to overconfidence because they do not believe the group can be valuable to them. Skillful counselors can reflect these discrepant emotions and caringly confront the peer teachers to promote recognition that these attitudes hinder professional improvement.

In the second stage new teachers begin to voice worries about their evaluations. They question whether these evaluations fairly represent their abilities. Counselors must reflect these anxious, insecure feelings while helping novice teachers to think more rationally about the evaluation process and understand how undue anxiety is blocking more appropriate behaviors (Thies-Sprinthall & Gerler, 1990).

As new teachers advance to more complex levels, a third stage emerges when they realize the similar concerns they have about classroom management. The facilitator helps them analyze specific reasons for successes or failures in classroom management and plan new strategies. Counselor challenges arising from this stage can spur novice teachers to consult with more experienced teachers, thus helping them to value professional collaboration for effective teaching (Thies-Sprinthall & Gerler, 1990).

The group will be well into the school year by the time some members have advanced to a fourth stage (Thies-Sprinthall & Gerler, 1990). At this stage they are more able to consider how their actions contribute to or hinder learning of their pupils. They can nondefensively solicit feedback from other faculty and take steps for changing lesson plans and activities. Instruction becomes a continuous quality improvement process.

Thies-Sprinthall and Gerler (1990) provide qualitative and quantitative evidence of the value of new teacher support groups for advancing their professional development. Empirical studies show gains in the capacity of new teachers to move from egocentric concerns to concerns about how teaching behaviors affect classroom management and pupil learning. Qualitative data from journal entries and leader observations supports the empirical findings. New teachers move from feelings of anxiety and isolation to a sense of community as they interact within the group. Gradually they are able to focus their energies outward and behave more flexibly and adequately in complex classroom situations. Wilkinson (1994) noted that by the end of the second semester her group had moved from discussing concrete concerns to expressing pride in their teaching styles, focusing their comments on ways to become more capable teachers.

Importance of Administrative Leadership

Administrative leadership is crucial for fulfilling the needs of novice teachers for both instructional and psychological support

(Buxton, 1996). An administrator must be willing to commit personnel, facilities, and resources in order to successfully implement new-teacher support groups.

The first time that a group is formed, school administrators should set forth clear expectations for attending a certain number of meetings and should also express anticipation for positive outcomes. When teachers have conflicts in their schedules, administrators can make suggestions about setting priorities. Advocating the support group establishes a vital link between the effort new teachers make to participate and the potential value of the support network to their own teaching. After a successful group has been in place for a year the members themselves will encourage others to attend (Wilkinson, 1994).

The counselor is an obvious choice as a group facilitator because he or she is not in an evaluative role, has been trained in consulting and group counseling, and has knowledge of human development and educational practices. In order to facilitate teacher development, counseling skills such as challenging and supporting behaviors are essential.

Before selecting a school counselor as the facilitator the administrator should consult with the counselor about how such a role would (a) affect the school counselor's other duties, (b) contribute to a nurturing school community, and (c) fit with the counselor's interests and personality. Because a well-run group contributes both to the development of the individual teacher and to the teaching-learning climate of the school, previously assigned duties may need to be reassigned in order to free the counselor to provide the needed leadership. Administrative support for the counselor's efforts comes through on-going consultation about the structure and direction of the group, as well as resource assistance in implementing changes which will benefit the new teachers.

Characteristics of Successful Groups

Successful groups begin and end on time. The leader must manage time effectively so that members have adequate time to process concerns. Together the members set the ground rules for maintaining confidentiality and treating members respectfully.

Although the facilitator provides a clear structure, teachers set their own agenda which is amended as the need arises. The facilitator invites everyone to participate, reflects feelings, clarifies content, caringly confronts, and ends the sessions on a positive note (Wilkinson, 1994).

Group meetings should last from 60 to 90 minutes, depending on the size of the group. Meeting on-site immediately after school is easier for the participants. Specifying regular times for the group to meet throughout the year works best, so that members can plan ahead. The authors found that members liked meeting at two week intervals during first semester and every three weeks during second semester. Members were expected to inform the leader when they would be absent. The leader kept records of attendees and contacted teachers who were absent to let them know they were missed (Wilkinson, 1994).

Meeting places should be comfortable, with space to place chairs or desks in a circle. Group size should be 10 to 15 members per leader in order for all members to have the chance for input at each meeting. Simple refreshments can be furnished by the members on a rotating basis, thus providing some "ownership" into the group.

Members may find it valuable to keep journals for personal reflection. Groups function as closed groups except when administrators or others are invited. Written evaluations allow feedback for planning and improving new groups. A celebration dinner or picnic provides valuable closure at the end of the year (Wilkinson, 1994).

Conclusion

A peer support group for beginning teachers facilitated by the school counselor is a valuable experience for the professional development of members. Serving as the group facilitator expands the counselor's role in promoting student development and provides a nucleus for fostering a nurturing climate in schools. Administrative support is necessary to make this counselor role a reality.

References

Buxton, J. B. (1996, Fall). Project Induct: A focus on beginning teachers and the profession of teaching. *Making Connections, 9,* 1. (Published by College of Education and Psychology, North Carolina State University, Raleigh, NC)

Hatfield, T., & Nelson, W. (1990, June). Developmental theory into practice in the schools: A vital counselor-principal partnership. *Journal of Counseling and Human Service Professions 4 (1),* 19-33.

Sprinthall, N. A., & Thies-Sprinthall, L. (1983). The teacher as an adult learner: A cognitive-developmental view. In G. Griffin (Ed.), *Staff Development* (NSSE Yearbook), (pp.13-35). Chicago: University of Chicago Press.

Thies-Sprinthall, L. M., & Gerler, E. R. (1990, Fall). Support groups for novice teachers. *Journal of Staff Development, 11 (4),* 18-22.

Wilkinson, C. M. (1994, Spring). Reflecting on experience: A support group for beginning educators. *The Delta Kappa Gamma Bulletin, 60 (3),* 41-45.

Charlotte M. Wilkinson-Speltz, Ed.D., NCC, NCSC is Associate Professor, Counselor Education Department, Winona State University, Winona, MN.

Edward Forsythe is Principal of the Durham Magnet Center for Visual and Performing Arts, Durham Public Schools, Durham, NC.

What A School Administrator Needs to Know About the School Counselor's Role in Organizational Team Building

Alan Basham, Valerie Appleton, & Cynthia Lambarth

Understanding the important contribution school counselors can make to the school team's effectiveness requires an awareness of two very basic but far-reaching facts. First, educational reform is creating major structural and systemic changes in schools and school districts across the nation. Management of educational organizations is shifting from a top-down, bureaucratic, hierarchical model to a site-based, community inclusive, team approach to policy setting, planning, and implementation (Glickman, 1993). For example, the largest school district in the authors' two communities has shifted from a hierarchical to a site-based management model in which a site council composed of parents, teachers, and school administrators at the local school now make many of the policy and planning decisions that were formerly made at the district or state level. These changes in how schools are run necessitate the presence of effective teams of community leaders, teachers, and administrators.

Second, the people who work at, or are actively interacting with local schools, are *people*. To create the conditions under which people can trust each other, work constructively to solve shared problems, and produce the best schools possible with the resources at hand, educators need more than ever to understand human nature in the organizational setting (Thatcher & Howard, 1989). Because school counselors are among the education professionals who understand best the relational needs, personality characteristics, and group dynamics that influence site teams, they are invaluable contributors to the construction of effective teams in the school setting.

In the current climate of educational reform, the role of the school counselor is shifting to include the organizational well-being of the school. While continuing to provide individual and group counseling for students, in addition to serving as a classroom ally to teachers, many school counselors are appropriately expanding their responsibilities to help create and maintain effective teams. Graduate programs in counselor education, accredited by The Council for Accreditation for Counseling and Related Educational Programs (CACREP) already require training in consultation, with an increasing emphasis placed on organizational development, conflict resolution, and team building. The focus of the school counselor is more and more on the dynamic of the teacher-parent-administrator team, helping to empower that team to reach its potential for the sake of students.

The Nature of Effective Teams

A team is a group of people whose relationship with each other is based on their efforts to accomplish a shared task (Johnson & Johnson, 1997). Three components characterize the most effective teams. First, the team members are committed to maintaining a constructive relational dynamic. Any team that gets the job done while creating adversarial relationships among people will eventually cause as many organizational problems as it solves. Second, an effective team has clearly established goals, roles, and methods. Everyone on the team knows what the task is, who is responsible for what, and how the team will actually get the job done. Third, the best teams consistently work at improving the first and second components; the status quo is never good enough for a great team.

A team's *functional effectiveness* is dependent on many factors, any one of which can reduce or destroy the team's efforts if not adequately addressed. These factors include

1. Positive interdependence among members, who learn to trust and depend on each other in an atmosphere of mutual respect.
2. Group processing skills, which enable team members to solve problems, resolve conflicts, and maintain a constructive relational dynamic.
3. Individual accountability, in which team members hold themselves and each other accountable for accomplishment of tasks and for influence on the organizational climate.
4. Promotive interaction, which encourages and facilitates others' efforts to achieve.

While there is no substitute for knowledge and ability in professional educators, without a constructive team dynamic the potential of a school's staff can never be fully reached (Burns, 1994). Team building, then, is a crucial component of creating a successful educational system, and no team is fully effective without honest, open, mutually supportive relationships among people. It is these working relationships among people that the school counselor is most equipped to help support and maintain.

Useful Counselor Skills

Counselors are trained to use group counseling skills in their interventions with students. Since most groups led by school counselors are topical in nature, the counselors use *group process* skills to help build trust and openness in the group while leading participants in a *discussion* about the topic at hand. These same skills are easily transferable to team building in the school setting. Counselors can help to build trust and openness among team members while leading a team discussion focused on making good decisions and finding workable solutions to school problems. The difference between team group process and counseling group process is that counseling groups focus on individual growth, while team building groups focus on improving team competence and accomplishing team tasks.

Most counselors also receive training in *conflict resolution* techniques as part of their graduate studies. Such mediational skills are directly applicable to resolving interpersonal and systemic conflicts that block team effectiveness.

Some organizational development consultants use *assessment* of personality type and working style of team members, synthesizing this information into a description of the group's shared dynamic. By presenting this insight to a working team, the counselor can increase the participants' understanding of differences in style that may be sources of conflict or confusion in the team. Helping team members in this way to understand, support, and rely on diversity instead of being frustrated by it, is a significant contribution that school counselors can make.

School counselors are trained to *listen* intently, to observe others' behavior, and to understand other perspectives. Besides modeling these skills, the school counselor can provide support and training as needed for school administrators and teachers. Improving active listening skills can facilitate positive interaction with parents, community leaders, and school employees.

Finally, most school counselor training programs stress the importance of *understanding* and *accepting* normal human nature. The best counselors are those who are committed to helping others grow, heal, and build character, while refusing to condemn or abandon them for their imperfections. While individual accountability is an integral part of any effective team, accepting and valuing others with an attitude of forgiveness is equally important. Most people thrive and do their best work in an atmosphere in which it is okay to err. Counselors are uniquely able to model and to champion this principle of organizational health.

Specific Tasks

School administrators and other leaders would do well to actively support the counselor's role in addressing the following needs at the local school. The school counselor can

1. Conduct workshops specifically designed to foster working alliances between parents and teachers. The format of such workshops should include opportunities for teachers and parents to talk with each other in small group settings. Such settings increase each participant's

understanding of the others' concerns, perspectives, and efforts.

2. Serve as a team building and advisory member of the site council or related community and administrative team of the school. The school counselor can have a significant constructive impact on the health of the leadership team if encouraged to help that team develop its potential.

3. Champion a constructive relational dynamic at the school by leading problem-solving, relationship building, or conflict resolution groups for the school staff.

4. Present informative staff development workshops on the nature of an effective team, clarification of organizational mission and leadership ethics, and enhancement of interpersonal relationships among co-workers, parents, and community leaders (Zamanou & Glaser, 1994). This activity can help to provide a common vision and sense of "us" which are essential for organizational health and success.

5. Help department heads (especially in secondary schools) work together to communicate effectively about cross-discipline education. Since students are motivated to learn when they understand the connections among their course work, teachers should be encouraged to provide those connections through a team effort (Parnell, 1994).

6. Conduct a program review of the organizational climate of the school setting, helping administrators to identify those areas of the organization that most need attention to maximize the school's potential.

Training

To serve in the capacity of team builder, some school counselors may need additional training. They should be encouraged to take course work in consultation, organizational development, and workshop preparation. Then all that is needed is the opportunity to implement the team building skills that the school counselor brings to the educational community.

Conclusion

Healthy organizations are those in which people have a high degree of job satisfaction and are intrinsically motivated to do their best work. The synergy that arises from positive interpersonal relationships and creative team efforts can help to produce a model school. Given the present stressors, political climate, and mandated changes affecting the educational system, creating a healthy team dynamic at your school may seem a daunting task. However, the authors believe that achieving such a dynamic is the key to thriving during this time of change and that school counselors are a major source of the information and ability needed to accomplish the task.

References

Burns, C. (1994). Innovative team building: Synergistic human resource development. *Administration and Policy in Mental Health, 22,* 39-48.

Glickman, C. (1993). *Renewing America's schools: A guide for school-based action.* San Francisco: Jossey-Bass.

Johnson, D., & Johnson, F. (1997). *Joining together: Group theory and group skills.* Boston, MA: Allyn & Bacon.

Parnell, D. (1994). *Logolearning: Searching for meaning in education.* Waco, TX: Center for Occupational Research and Development, Inc.

Thatcher, J., & Howard, M. (1989). Enhancing professional effectiveness: Management training for the head teacher. *Educational and Child Psychology, 6,* 45-50.

Zamanou, S., & Glaser, S. (1994). Moving toward participation and involvement: Managing and measuring organizational culture. *Group & Organization Management, 19,* 475-502.

Alan Basham is Senior Lecturer of Applied Psychology at Eastern Washington University, Cheney, WA.

Valerie Appleton is Associate Professor of Applied Psychology and Director of Counselor Education at Eastern Washington University, Cheney, WA.

Cynthia Lambarth is Associate Superintendent of the Spokane Public School District (No. 81) in Spokane, WA.

What a School Administrator Needs to Know About *How to Evaluate a School Counselor*

Pamela Tucker, James Stronge, & Carol Beers

Once hired, school counselors present a distinct challenge in terms of supervision and evaluation. The role expectations for school counselors include both instructional and administrative components but these can vary significantly depending on the settings and audiences. Principals are faced with the dilemma of what criteria to use in the evaluation process to ensure fairness and utility. Based on the considerable research and professional literature from the field of counseling, we have outlined an evaluation process which is straightforward, flexible, and reflective of the professional standards for school counselors. Specifically, we have described a field-tested evaluation model that includes criteria for evaluation and methodology for collecting performance information. As with evaluation for all school personnel, evaluation of counselors is most effective when it is based on mutual respect and open communication, and it is integrated into the overall goals of the school.

The *Goals and Roles Evaluation Model,* as illustrated in Figure 1., reflects an evaluation cycle consisting of six distinct steps. The Development Phase, consisting of the first three steps, is primarily

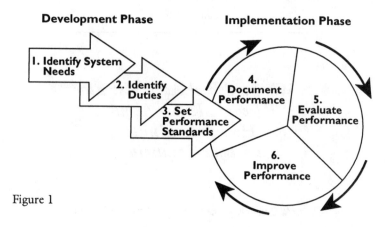

Goals & Roles Evaluation Model

Development Phase

Implementation Phase

1. Identify System Needs

2. Identify Duties

3. Set Performance Standards

4. Document Performance

5. Evaluate Performance

6. Improve Performance

Figure 1

a one-time exercise to develop the evaluation system and would need to be "revisited" only periodically in order to update the system in light of changes in the school's needs, the program, or the counselor's position. The Implementation Phase of the *Goals and Roles Model*, consisting of steps four through six, reflects a continual cycle of evaluation designed to promote opportunities for both school improvement and individual performance improvement.

Step 1: Identify System Needs

The purpose of step one is to identify the needs both of the school system and of the individual school through the examination of the current counseling program and personnel, and by the assessment of future needs. Many school systems have developed mission statements and strategic plans that reflect not only the current status of programs and personnel, but also the identified needs and priorities of the community. These documents, along with goal statements specific to the counseling program, provide a logical foundation for the definition of individual counselor roles in the achievement of the school's goals. Evaluation reasonably can be defined as the process of determining value relative to stated objectives. Therefore, determining the needs of the school is a prerequisite for all remaining steps if the

60

evaluation process is to be relevant to the school's mission and, ultimately, accountable to the public. This relevance becomes possible by translating goals into operational terms.

Step 2: Develop Roles

Translating program expectations into professional roles and responsibilities is the means by which the goals of the school and counseling program are operationalized for personnel evaluation. Fortunately, there is ample guidance from national organizations such as the American School Counselor Association on the definition of professionally appropriate and relevant responsibilities for school counselors. But no matter how large or small the school system, it is important to define responsibilities through a collaborative process, involving school counselors, principals, and others, in which a clear direction for the program, the evaluation process, and the evaluated personnel are determined. Just as the assessed needs of the school serve to clarify the expectations of all programs, the counseling program expectations serve to define the professional responsibilities of school counselors. Program goals, such as the provision of preventive counseling services, need to be translated into duties such as "uses appropriate assessment and diagnostic procedures for implementing counseling services."

Drawing upon numerous sources, the following delineation of major responsibilities might define the primary responsibilities for a school counselor.

Planning/Administration:
1. Structures the counseling programs by needs assessment, goal setting, planning, implementation, and evaluation procedures.
2. Manages time effectively and provides services on schedule.
3. Implements and coordinates school-wide counseling services and activities.
4. Provides specialized services for students.
5. Maintains an organized, functional, current counseling center.

Assessment/Evaluation:
1. Interprets testing results.
2. Assesses attainment of counseling program objectives.

Intervention/Direct Services:
1. Provides individual and group counseling services to meet the developmental, preventive, and remedial needs of students.
2. Uses appropriate assessment and diagnostic procedures for implementing counseling services.
3. Provides follow-up activities to monitor student progress.
4. Demonstrates the ability to organize and integrate the precollegiate/post-high school guidance and counseling component into the total school guidance program.

Collaboration:
1. Presents instructional/informational programs to groups of students, parents, teachers, and other school and community personnel.
2. Consults with students, parents, and school staff to assist in meeting student needs.
3. Seeks input from school staff concerning functioning of school counseling program.
4. Serves as an advocate for all students.
5. Serves as liaison between school and community agencies.
6. Assists with coordination of student services in the school.
7. Assists teachers with integration of guidance activities into the curriculum.
8. Conducts in-service training for faculty and staff.

Professional Responsibilities and Personal Development:
1. Adheres to ethical standards of the counseling profession.
2. Carries out professional responsibilities.
3. Upgrades professional knowledge and skills.

Step 3: Set Performance Standards

Setting performance standards provides an opportunity for schools to establish a predetermined level of desired or acceptable performance and expected outcomes. Determining and setting standards for school counselors will be specific to a particular school based on the needs of the program, and the availability of resources, facilities, and time. Standards also need to reflect the purpose(s) of the specific position. To be appropriate and valid, performance standards must establish realistic criteria for evaluation based on the resources, or lack thereof, in a given setting. Standards address *how well* a job is to be done, *how often* it is to be done, and ultimately *whether* it is done at all. Standards can be used to determine acceptable versus unacceptable levels of performance (a two-tiered rating system), or to distinguish multiple levels of acceptable behavior extending up to exemplary or exceptional. Although the former option is less time-consuming, the latter provides a framework for achievement, recognition, and professional development.

Step 4: Document Job Performance

Once the Development Phase is complete, the Implementation Phase begins with the collecting of factual descriptions of the counselor's behavior or performance to the fullest extent possible. Documenting job performance should be seen as a collaborative process with input from the school counselor and, to some extent, from all parties affected. This process could include principal(s), central office staff, teachers, subordinates, and students, depending on the nature of the counselor's roles and responsibilities. There are many options for documenting performance other than the traditional observation used extensively for teacher evaluation. These options include

1. self-assessment (rating forms, narratives, videotapes, etc.);
2. document review (program plans, implementation strategies, budgets, activity summaries, etc.);
3. client surveys (students, teachers, etc.);
4. peer assessment;

5. performance portfolios.

These alternative information collection strategies shift some of the responsibility for accountability and professional development to the school counselor. This approach to evaluation is a move away from the traditional inspection model of evaluation and is a more professionalizing approach to performance evaluation. Moreover, the use of multiple data sources in the evaluation process provides a fairer, more ethical and valid system of evaluating school counselors. Ultimately, through the use of this process, the principal is able to make informed summative judgments about the comprehensive responsibilities of the school counselor and the school counselor has the opportunity to take a more active role in the evaluation process.

Step 5: Evaluate Performance

Step five involves the comparison of documented job performance with established standards. The vehicle for this crucial step in the evaluation process is typically the evaluation conference. The conference provides a forum where the measurement of a person's documented job performance and achievements is compared with previously established goals and objectives, using established standards for measuring the level of that performance. The difference between the standards and the performance is known as a "discrepancy analysis." What to do with the discrepancy depends on the purpose of the evaluation as well as the degree of the discrepancy. If the evaluation has been formative in nature, it is used to restructure, improve, or modify the evaluatee's performance. If the evaluation has been summative, further improvement becomes only one of a variety of possible decisions and actions. It should be noted, however, that for personnel evaluation to be most meaningful and effective, both formative (i.e., improvement oriented) and summative (i.e., decision oriented) purposes should be included.

Step 6: Improve and Maintain Professional Service

The purpose of the final step is to provide recognition for

noteworthy performance and to offer corrective feedback for performance improvement. Improving and maintaining professional service may take the form of a variety of personnel decisions, including assisting personnel in improving their performance, personnel transfers, and, when necessary, termination. This step suggests the importance of professional development that balances the interests of the individual and the interests of the school. Moreover, the hallmark of an effective performance evaluation system is ongoing communication and regular feedback within an environment of mutual respect and trust.

Step six brings the evaluation process full circle by using the results of the discrepancy analysis in step five to improve or maintain professional service. For those counselors who meet or exceed established standards, step six provides an opportunity to discuss maintaining the current level of productivity or to identify new goals or higher levels of proficiency in achieving current ones. For counselors who do not meet established standards, it is important to analyze the reasons why a discrepancy exists. In some cases, goals and standards may be unrealistic given the available resources and circumstances. If the counselor has failed to meet reasonable goals and standards, the discrepancy analysis provides a diagnosis of specific problems with job performance. This information is helpful in developing a plan for improvement and remediation (which would involve another cycle of steps four, five, and six).

Conclusion

This capsule described how principals and counselors can develop and implement meaningful and effective evaluations. Along with the six-step *Goals and Roles Evaluation Model*, which defines a process for evaluation, specific suggestions were made for evaluation criteria and methods of gathering performance information.

Pamela Tucker, Ed.D., is Assistant Professor of Leadership, Foundations, and Policy, University of Virginia, Charlottesville, VA.

James Stronge, Ph.D., is Heritage Professor and Area Coordinator of Educational Policy, Planning, and Leadership, College of William and Mary, Williamsburg, VA.

Carol Beers, Ed.D., is Assistant Superintendent of Williamsburg-James City County Schools, Williamsburg, VA.

What a School Administrator Needs to Know About *How to Hire a School Counselor*

Cass Dykeman, Jim Dykeman, & Bob Pedersen

In the professional life of a school principal, few hiring decisions outrank the importance of the counselor hire. A good counselor can make any principal's life inestimably easier. In contrast, poor counselor hires can make any principal's work load even more demanding. Given the high stakes nature of counselor hires, we have detailed in this capsule a hiring approach that can maximize a principal's chances of making a good hiring decision. Specifically, we have outlined a seven-step approach that is both doable and effective. This approach incorporates hiring practices used by professionals in the executive search consultant industry. We wrote this capsule for the principal acting as the sole hiring agent. However, the techniques contained in this capsule are equally doable by a principal alone or by a principal with a hiring committee.

Step I: Articulate Hiring Needs

The first thing you must do when faced with a counselor hiring decision is articulate what needs you are trying to meet for your school through this hire. Without such an articulation, the entire hiring process will become rudderless. Why? For the average school counseling position, there may be many applicants who meet the basic hiring requirements (e.g., proper degree, certification, and work experience). Yet, without an investigation and articulation of the counseling needs of your particular building, your hire may duplicate current strengths and further exacerbate current weaknesses. For example, a high school may have a position open that was vacated by the counseling staff member who took a special interest in the students who had been in drug abuse treatment. Over the years, this counselor would check on these vulnerable students and make sure they were keeping up on their school work and following their aftercare program. The other counseling staff members may have little interest or perceived self-efficacy in working with these students. Thus, a prudent principal will informally survey counselors, parents, teachers, and students to find out the needs an open counseling position must fill (e.g., a counselor who likes to work with drug involved students). After collecting a list of needs, you should rank them. The needs should be ranked in order of importance to the specific mission of your school. This ranking should guide the hiring process beyond the determination of basic qualifications.

Step II: Recruit for Best Applicants

Ironically, the best applicants for any open position are typically people not currently seeking a position. Specifically, school counselors who (a) are doing a great job working at another school in your area, and (b) would be open to the professional opportunities that your school could provide that their present school does not. For example, your school adheres to a comprehensive, developmental school counseling model. Schools following this model allow counselors more time for activities such as group counseling and classroom presentations. Thus, schools using this model are going to be very attractive to achievement-oriented counselors who, at their present school, still must perform clerical tasks (e.g., class registration).

How do you find achievement-oriented applicants? The answer is "indirect recruiting." Indirect recruiting occurs in three stages. These stages are as follows:

Stage One: Solicit from principals, counselors, and teachers the names of counselors "who are leaders in the field."

Stage Two: Call the identified counselors and do the following: (a) Tell the counselor that he or she has been identified as a leader in the counseling field; (b) Tell the counselor that you are seeking his or her help; (c) Describe the position and its positive career path opportunities; and (d) Ask the counselor for the names of possible applicants who he or she thinks you should have a conversation with about this position.

Stage Three: One of two things will happen in Stage Two: (a) The counselor will give you the names of other counselors; or (b) The counselor will tell you that he or she may be interested in the position. If (a) occurs, repeat Stage Two with these new counselors. If (b) occurs, describe the position's opportunities again and detail for the counselor how he or she may apply.

Step III: The Paper Screen

Compared with the indirect recruiting approach, the traditional advertise-and-paper screen approach is less effective. Why? Application files only contain an applicant's "features." By features we mean an applicant's degree, school, g.p.a., position, etc. The problem with a features-only approach is that it does not reveal what an applicant actually *does* when working as a counselor. Specifically, can the applicant show quantifiable accomplishments? For example, how did the counselor work to improve the students' academic performance? Wise principals examine both an applicant's "features" *and* "accomplishments."

However, the world is not perfect. Therefore, what should you do if you can only conduct a paper screening before face-to-face interviews? Even in this less than optimal situation, you should still look for hints of an applicant's accomplishments. Moreover, the presence of accomplishment data in an applicant's file serves as a positive indicator of a counselor's achievement orientation.

Recent graduates, also can be good applicants. The drawback to this type of applicant is that showing a string of quantifiable accomplishments is more difficult for them. Ask recent graduates for quantifiable accomplishments from their internship and from their non-education related employment. Recent graduates who attended CACREP accredited counselor training programs deserve a special look. CACREP is the national accrediting body for counselor training programs. CACREP accredited programs tend to be longer and they involve more extensive supervision than the average counselor training program. As such, these programs demand more of a commitment on the part of the student. Thus, attendance at a CACREP accredited program hints at the achievement orientation of the applicant.

Step IV: Reference Checks

Using the steps detailed above, you should identify three to five applicants whose features and accomplishments best suggest that they will meet your school's needs. Now it is time to check the references of these applicants. Profitable reference checking occurs in two stages. First, ask each applicant for the names and phone numbers of three present or former supervisors. Also ask that each applicant contact these supervisors and let them know that (a) you will be calling, and (b) you have the applicant's permission to talk to the supervisor. Second, call the supervisors and ask questions that "pull" for descriptions of the applicant's quantifiable accomplishments. Please note that one bad reference should *not* knock an applicant out of consideration. If an applicant gets a bad reference, ask for three more former supervisor references and call these references.

Step V: The Hiring Interview

In both American education and industry, most hiring authorities conduct *opinion-based* rather than *behavior-based* interviews. The problem with opinion-based interviews is that they are poor predictors of what an applicant will actually do in a position. The best predictor of future success is past success. Thus, your interview questions should be behavior-based. Specifically, you should ask for examples of quantifiable accomplishments in areas where you have identified your needs. For instance, one of your needs is to cut your drop-out rate. If so, the following string of questions would be appropriate:

> *Q. #1:* Ms. Smith, please give me an example of an intervention that you conducted to cut the drop-out rate at Riverbend High School? Most likely, they will answer this question in the following way: "Well, I designed and ran three small groups for students at-risk for dropping out." You should follow-up this answer with an even narrower behavior-based question such as Q. #2.

> *Q. #2:* "Ms. Smith, what percentage of the students in the groups you lead dropped out of school within one year?" As you can probably sense, behavior-based questioning provides a robust sense of an applicant's achievement history and orientation. For instance, contrast Q. #1 with the related opinion-based question: "Ms. Smith, what can counselors do to ease the drop-out rate?" Which of these two questions will best pull the information you really need to make a sound hiring decision?

Step VI: The Observation

Following a behavior-based interview, you should observe each applicant "in-action." Observations can provide you another valuable data-point on what an applicant will *actually do* as a counselor. The type of observation you conduct should vary given the level and needs of your school. For example, you may need a counselor that can help teachers with classroom behavior problems. Thus, you can set up an observation where each applicant conducts a five minute consult with a teacher. The teacher and the problem should stay the same across applicants. As an aside, be sure to ask the teacher you used for their opinion on the applicants. Observation participants can provide a valuable alternative perspective on applicants.

Step VII: The Offer and Close

OK, you have rank ordered the acceptable applicants. Now, how do you "land" the applicant you want most? First, the key thing to remember about this stage is that "time kills all deals." Thus, a principal should be prepared to move crisply to hire after the final face-to-face interview. Second, all acceptable applicants should receive a phone call within 24 hours of their face-to-face interview. The purpose of this phone call is to give feedback concerning the interview. Why should you make this phone call? Without any feedback, applicants will read negatives into their interview performance. Over time, these negatives will lead applicants to rationalize why the position is the wrong one for them.

When it comes time to make the offer, you should remember that your highest ranked applicant probably either (a) already works as a counselor, or (b) has a choice between many open positions. Thus, you must be prepared to highlight for the applicant how the growth opportunities the applicant seeks are present in the position you have open. Why is this highlighting necessary? It is necessary because professionals predominately switch jobs in order to expand their opportunities. Now, what if all of your acceptable applicants reject your employment offer? If this unfortunate circumstance happens, you should sit down and revisit how you have structured counseling in your school. Specifically, you should ask yourself the question: How can I restructure this position so that high achieving counselors will be attracted to it? The other capsules in this series can help you answer this question.

Conclusion

This capsule described how principals can improve their counselor hirings. Specifically, this capsule detailed an efficient seven-step process that increases the probability of hiring the applicant with the best chance for success.

Cass Dykeman, Ph.D., NCC, NCSC, MAC is Associate Professor of Applied Psychology and Director of School Counseling, Eastern Washington University, Cheney, WA.

Jim Dykeman is President of Management Recruiters of Mercer Island, Mercer Island, WA.

Bob Pedersen is Principal of Woodridge Elementary School, Spokane, WA.

What a School Administrator Needs to Know About the School Counselor's Role With Academic Advisement

Robert S. Tobias & Robert L. Harbach

Introduction

Any discussion on the school counselor's role with academic advisement needs to begin with a review of basic terms. The terms "counselor" and "counseling" according to common dictionary definitions are as follows:

1. **Counselor**: Advisor.
2. **Counseling:** The professional guidance of the individual by using psychological methods especially in collecting case history data, using various techniques of the personal interview, and testing interests and aptitudes.

Many trained and talented professionals inhabit educational institutions, for example, school teachers. They impart knowledge, foster a desire to learn, and train for the various disciplines. Also, many teachers have remarkable humanistic attributes that enable them to perceive and address individual student needs. However, teachers face a daily grind of lesson planning, instructional presentations, and student progress evaluations. Thus, it is the school counselor, unencumbered by these duties, who is best equipped to help individual students establish short- and long-range personal and educational goals.

The Academic Advisor Role

Whether in an individual or a group setting, counselors need to be provided with tools that effectively help them to serve in the academic advisor role. The first critical tool is a clear set of counseling policies and procedures. This tool gives counselors operational safeguards against possible litigation. Another critical tool is client confidentiality. The ability to maintain confidentiality enables the counselor to help students deal with matters of consequence.

A final critical tool is information. In this computer generation, most school districts have a central data bank for input, update, storage, and retrieval of student records. Counselor access to these information service tools is no longer a luxury. Each counselor needs to be able to obtain information as the need dictates. This is of particular significance where students move from school to school within a large school district, or transfer in from other school districts. Dealing with human emotion, which is in part what counselors do, requires as much detailed preparation as does the physician before recommending medical treatment. School administrators can help a school realize its mission of the school by serving as the catalyst that enables the counselor to be equipped with materials, information, and time needed to advise students.

The Use of Testing in Academic Advising

School administrators are accountable to the school district, parents, and the community for making site-based decisions concerning the educational placement and success of enrolled students. The value of test results in this decision-making process is widely accepted. What remain open questions are the "who," "when," and "what" to test, as well as who does the testing. In addition, there are instances when the administrator has no option for test selection. For example, in Nevada all graduating students must pass the Nevada State High School Proficiency Exam to qualify for a traditional high school diploma.

By establishing and maintaining a collegial and collaborative working relationship with teachers and counselors, the administrator garners support and assistance necessary for the successful execution of the test-giving activities. The availability of systems for rapid scoring and reporting of test results enables counselors to apply this information. Counselors have been trained in the use of test results. They know how to blend student test scores, student academic history, student extra-class experiences, and student conference information into strategies for helping students develop short-term and long-term goals.

Registration and Scheduling
and the Role of the Academic Advisor

The terms "student registration" and "student enrollment" are often used interchangeably. Some persons interpret registration to be the initial entrance by a student into the records of a school, or school district, whereas enrollment is viewed as when the student first reports to class. The term registration, as used here, deals with the student completing the process that makes him or her a member of the school, or school district student population. There are probably as many variations to the mechanics for student registration as there are secondary schools. The numbers and kinds of staff involved in the registration process is usually a product of the size of the school. In some instances a student's initial registration is maintained throughout his or her high school career. Schools that experience a transient student population may find student registration to be a continuous process.

Many things happen at a school before students are registered. Administrative decisions need to be made that determine course offerings, staff assignments, school hours, what the school expects of students, and what the students can expect of the school.

School counselors are a valuable resource when serving as part of the administrative team that establishes the school's direction. By virtue of their interaction with colleagues at feeder schools, by keeping abreast of post-secondary education and employment opportunities, and by maintaining communication with students and parents, counselors can provide practical ideas for determining curriculum priorities.

The counselor's role in the registration process is most

effective as the person who helps the student develop his or her schedule. Many large schools have a menu of generic four year schedules from which students can choose and initiate their studies. Experience has shown that many students entering high school have predetermined personal educational goals. This is especially true for college-bound students. The student/counselor working alliance is important in ensuring that courses taken by the student satisfy the eligibility and entrance requirements at the college or university of choice. Students who have not yet established a personal preference or direction may be initially scheduled into those classes required for high school graduation. Important counselor activities, which merit administrative support and encouragement, are to arrange follow-up sessions that guide the students through a variety of exploratory activities leading to the selection of a more meaningful and appropriate schedule of classes.

The development of a four-year plan for each student is the ideal. The reality is that students deviate by failing classes, changing goals, withdrawing from one school and enrolling in another, and by dropping out for a semester, or longer. Counselors strive to keep current with their students. Their ability to recommend and develop appropriate student schedules is an asset for the school. As a spin-off from the scheduling activities, counselors can advise administrators about the success and viability of programs and teachers.

There are times when students seek certain classes and they actually avoid certain classes. During the scheduling process, counselors are made very much aware of this. Without perceiving themselves as program evaluators, counselors should be encouraged to report this to the school administrator. If the class in question is a required subject, the administrator may choose to investigate the reasons for such student attitudes. In the case of an elective subject, consideration may be given to the relevance of the class as part of the mission of the school.

Conclusion

Each school administrator is charged with the orchestration of the many variables that are necessary for the realization of the school's mission. The successes attained by students is a measure of how well the mission is accomplished. School counselors have their fingers on the pulse of the school. They are continuously in contact with students, parents, and staff. Counselors need to decide if and how to share information with the administrator — information that has value to the improvement of the good and welfare of the school and of the student population overall.

As an academic advisor, the counselor promotes the concept of the school's mission, encourages students to strive for success with established classes and assignments, and attempts to help staff better understand student strengths and deficiencies. As an interpreter of data, the counselor accesses and utilizes test scores, achievement grades, and interest surveys to help students select the educational direction most appropriate for them at the moment. As a participant in the development of the school curriculum, the counselor shares information on programs that are fruitful and those that fall short of desired student outcomes.

One of the Caesars attributed his success to "standing on the shoulders of giants." The school counselors are among the giants available to the school administrator.

Robert S. Tobias is Site Administrator at Sunset High West in Las Vegas, NV.

Robert L. Harbach is Associate Professor in the Department of Educational Psychology, University of Nevada, Las Vegas, NV.

What a School Administrator Needs to Know About the School Counselor's Role With Career Development

Spencer G. Niles & J. Andrew Stamp

School counselors focus on providing systematic and comprehensive career development services to students in grades K–12. The National Occupational Information Coordinating Committee (NOICC) created the "National Career Development Guidelines" (1989) to identify the career assistance that students require at each level of schooling. Specifically, students need assistance in: (1) increasing self-knowledge; (2) educational and occupational exploration; and (3) lifelong career planning (NOICC, 1989). Essentially, assistance in these areas is provided throughout elementary, middle, and senior high school.

Career development programs at the elementary school level increase students' self and career awareness. Students in grades K–5 are exposed to different types of career opportunities and are helped to understand the relationship between self-characteristics (e.g., interests, values, strong academic and interpersonal skills) and various occupational requirements. Students also learn effective decision-making skills at the elementary school level.

Middle school students strive to become more sophisticated in their self and career awareness. They learn more about the importance of (a) developing a positive self-concept; (b) developing interpersonal and academic skills; (c) the relationship between school subjects and work requirements; (d) how to locate and use occupational information; (e) how to seek and obtain a job; (f) how discriminatory attitudes constrain career development; and (g) how to engage in systematic career exploration and planning.

Students in senior high school begin the process of more formal career planning by increasing their understanding of the interrelationships of intellectual, emotional, physical, and career development. They also learn about factors that are necessary to consider in career decision-making (e.g., values, training requirements). They begin the process of choosing and implementing tentative career decisions (e.g., by selecting a curriculum of study, pursuing part-time work, or becoming involved in volunteer activities).

The Role of the School Counselor

Counselors facilitate students' career development by providing direct and indirect services to students. Counselors offer direct services to students by providing individual and group career planning experiences (often through the on-going use of educational and career planning portfolios), classroom career guidance (which focuses on providing a wide array of occupational and educational information to students), and career assessment activities (most often related to interests, skills, and values assessment). In these experiences, counselors typically seek to (a) increase students' self-and occupational- awareness; (b) help students understand the connection between school and work; and (c) encourage students to take an active and informed role in their own career planning.

Counselors also empower others so that they can provide effective career assistance to students (Herr & Niles, 1994). For example, counselors offer indirect services to students by including teachers and parents/guardians in the career development program. In fact, the success of any career development program is largely dependent on helping teachers and parents identify ways they can foster career development in their students and children.

Counselors help teachers foster career development in their students by identifying strategies that teachers can use to infuse the curriculum with career concepts, so that students are able to connect academic experiences with future work experiences. An excellent list of career development activities teachers can use is provided in Herr and Cramer (1996). To help parents foster career development in their children, counselors teach parents about effective strategies for managing career development concerns (e.g., how to identify appropriate occupational options, how to get a job, how to communicate effectively in the workplace). Herr and Niles (1994) offer a number of useful suggestions as to how parents can become actively involved in the career development of their children.

Finally, counselors develop linkages between the school and the community by involving employers and community leaders in the delivery of career development services to students. Employers and community leaders become involved in the delivery of career services by serving as role models and by mentoring students. This is accomplished within the context of classroom presentations, part-time employment experiences, internships, externships (i.e., job shadowing opportunities), and volunteer activities.

Resistance to and Benefits of Career Development Programs

Comments typically made in discussions related to providing systematic and comprehensive career development assistance to students are: "Sounds good, but who has the time or money to provide career development activities to students?" and "I'd like to help students with their career development, but I have to focus on academic success!" Such comments assume that providing career assistance to students is time consuming, costly, and unrelated to academic achievement.

While it is true that providing a systematic and comprehensive career development program requires counselors, teachers, and parents/guardians to invest their time, the amount of time required is often not as significant as many imagine. Additionally, much of the time that is required involves the "start-up" time required in planning and initiating a systematic and comprehensive career development program. Moreover, the time and cost required in the planning stage can be reduced by drawing upon effective career development resources that have already been developed and delineated elsewhere (see Herr & Cramer, 1996). Thus, most of the resources (goals, activities, materials, and personnel) needed for delivering career services are already in place.

Of course, whether time and money should be invested in providing career assistance to students depends upon the benefits that can be expected from such programs. The findings of numerous literature reviews (e.g., Crites, 1987; Herr, 1982; Herr & Cramer, 1996; Spokane & Oliver, 1983) suggest that providing students with career development assistance is a wise investment. Isaacson and Brown (1997, p. 264) summarize these research findings noting that as a result of receiving career assistance, students can expect to have a more positive self-concept, better social skills, stronger decision-making skills, improved academic achievement (including better retention and attendance rates), increased motivation due to the identification of personal career goals, and a better understanding of the relationship between school and work. Parents become more involved in the educational and career planning of their children, and schools achieve greater accountability as a result of the documentation acquired in the on-going career planning process.

Despite these demonstrated benefits, many schools have not initiated systematic and comprehensive career development programs. Administrative support is a key factor in establishing such programs. By working collaboratively with school counselors, school administrators can provide a catalyst for instituting systematic and comprehensive career development programs aimed at helping all students maximize their opportunities for success in school and beyond.

References

Crites, J. O. (1987). *Evaluation of career guidance programs: Models, methods, and microcomputers.* Columbus, OH: NCRVE, Ohio State University.

Herr, E. L. (1982). The effects of guidance and counseling: Three domains. In E. L. Herr & N. M. Pinson (Eds.), *Foundations of policy in guidance and counseling* (pp. 22-64). Alexandria, VA: American Association of Counseling and Development.

Herr, E. L., & Cramer, S. H. (1996). *Career guidance and counseling through the lifespan: Systematic approaches* (5th ed.). New York: Harper Collins.

Herr, E. L., & Niles, S. G. (1994). Multicultural career guidance in the schools. In P. Pederson & J. Carey (Eds.), *Multicultural counseling in schools.* (pp. 177-194). Boston: Allyn and Bacon.

Isaacson, L. E., & Brown, D. (1997). *Career information, career counseling, and career development.* Boston: Allyn and Bacon.

NOICC. (1989). *The national career development guidelines: Local handbook for high schools.* Washington, DC: Author.

Spokane, A. R., & Oliver, L. W. (1983). The outcomes of vocational intervention. In S. H. Osipow & B. Walsh (Eds.), *Handbook of Vocational Psychology,* Vol. 2. Hillsdale, NJ: Erlbaum.

Spencer G. Niles is an Associate Professor of Counselor Education, University of Virginia, Charlottesville, VA.

J. Andrew Stamp is Assistant Executive Director of the Virginia Association of School Superintendents, Charlottesville, VA.

Chapter 13

What a School Administrator Needs to Know About the Use of *Graduate Interns, Teacher Advisors, Peer Facilitators, and Paraprofessionals in Guidance Services*

John A. Casey & Penny Chennell

All counselors are alike. . . or, are they?

As budgets tighten, needs soar, and demands for restructuring increase, administrators are challenged to find creative ways to offer effective counseling and guidance services for the least expense. Many consider the use of graduate students, teacher advisors, peer facilitators, and paraprofessionals as cost effective alternatives to hiring additional professional school counselors. Although not interchangeable with trained school counselors, these guidance personnel can be important assets in a comprehensive guidance program. But not without careful planning.

Graduate Interns

The most common source of graduate students is the local university training program. Typically, students are placed by the university in conjunction with a formal course (i.e., practicum and internship). The Council for Accreditation of Counseling and Related Educational Programs (CACREP, 1994) requires students in accredited programs to complete 100 clock hours of supervised practicum followed by 600 hours of supervised internship. Professional liability insurance, in conjunction with membership in a professional organization, is often expected of the student by the university. Training programs accredited by CACREP require a minimum of 48 to 60 semester hours for the master's degree.

Comprehensive university counselor education programs may offer training specialties in many concentrations. These specialties include (a) School Counseling; (b) Community or Agency Counseling; (c) Marriage, Family and Child Counseling; (d) Rehabilitation Counseling; (e) Career Counseling; (f) Gerontological Counseling; and (g) Student Services in Higher Education. Principals often mistakenly assume these specialties are interchangeable; they are not. *School Counseling* students are selected and trained in conjunction with agreements with state departments of education. Thus, they often have teacher credentials and/or classroom experience and are trained to work with students, parents, teachers, and staff within the school culture. Counseling interns and even counseling professors *without* School Counseling training can create problems within the school through ignorance of school law, failure to act within school regulations, poor classroom management, or inappropriate consultation. One costly lawsuit can negate otherwise well-intentioned attempts by administrators at cost savings, particularly when a disaffected parent is angry, looking for a scapegoat, and targeting the "deep pockets" of a school district.

The American School Counselor Association (ASCA, 1984) has established a set of ethical standards for school counselor interns and professionals. These include: "The school counselor functions within the boundaries of individual professional competencies and accepts responsibility for his/her actions" and "The school counselor monitors personal functioning and effectiveness and refrains from any activity that may lead to inadequate professional services or harm to a client." Since administrators assume significant legal responsibility for paid or unpaid graduate students at a school site, careful screening procedures that consider CACREP and ASCA guidelines are important. The following questions might typically be asked by an administrator prior to placement of graduate students at the school site:

- *For the graduate student:*

Have you ever been convicted of a felony or misdemeanor? What courses have you successfully completed with K–12 applications? What school-based experience have you had? Will you provide proof of professional liability insurance? What training have you received in school law and ethics issues, including confidentiality and child abuse reporting? When do you know it is time to consult and refer?

- *For the university faculty member:*

Does your program follow CACREP guidelines for the training of school counselors? What is the ratio of faculty to students in field supervision? What K–12 experience have you had in field supervision? How does training for counselors who will work in schools, differ from training for other specialties? How will crises be handled? How will legal, ethical, or competence questions be addressed?

- *For the school counselor serving as site supervisor:*

What training have you had in supervision theory and practice? How will time for supervision be scheduled? How will crises be handled? How will legal, ethical, or competence questions be addressed? Will you develop a written contract specifying expectations from all involved? Are the assigned duties within the graduate student's scope of competence? If audio or videotaping is involved, how will permission be obtained? Will clients be explicitly informed of the difference between services provided by the graduate student and the professional counselor?

Teacher Advisors

Encouraged by school reform advocates, teacher advisement programs have been widely incorporated in school restructuring as an extension of the school guidance program. These programs have been described as a supporting ongoing relationship between a student and a caring adult, which provides the student with security, advice, affirmation, and a positive role model (California Commission on Teacher Credentialing, 1996).

Administrators must understand and clearly delineate the

boundary between *guidance curriculum* practiced by teacher advisors and *counseling activities* practiced by professional school counselors. Advisory programs are based on curriculums designed to promote healthy skills for coping with normal developmental challenges; they are not substitutes for counseling interventions with more serious needs. The California Commission on Teacher Credentialing (1996) has drafted a document with a stern caution about these boundaries, warning that teachers may provide useful support to students but are not trained to deal with serious personal and psychological problems. It further states that individuals who may be well meaning, but not professionally prepared, may give injurious advice and may not recognize the seriousness of a student's problem, leading to significant damage to the student.

In a well-constructed teacher advisory program, a developmentally targeted guidance curriculum, voluntary teacher involvement, ongoing inservice, and appropriate school counselor supervision and consultation can enhance the teacher/learner relationship while providing for counseling referral when warranted.

Peer Facilitators

Peer assistance programs, facilitated by school-age peer facilitators (also known as peer helpers, peer counselors, or natural helpers), have grown dramatically in recent years. One motivation for adopting peer programs is the assumption that students are more likely to share concerns with peers long before sharing them with adults. Numerous commercial programs have been developed to assist in the training of peer facilitators and have yielded many success stories, as reported by school personnel. Even peer programs, however, can be ticking time bombs when organized without trained counselors.

A comprehensive survey by Lewis and Lewis (1996) reviewed published articles and practitioner experiences about peer assistance programs. Their survey yielded responses from 263 individuals working in 305 schools (K–12) reporting on data from 1991–1993 in the state of Washington. One disturbing finding, discovered by the authors, is the statistically significant disproportionate rate of "successful" suicides in schools where peer assistance programs were supervised by teachers or administrators rather than by trained professional counselors. Specifically, their extrapolated data projected a rate of 15.4 suicides per 100,000 students annually in teacher- or administrator-led programs; 8.4 suicides per 100,000 students annually in schools where no peer program existed, and 5.4 suicides per 100,000 students annually in schools where pupil-personnel-led (i.e., counselor, school psychologist, or school social worker) peer programs existed. Although the authors caution that further study is warranted, they also conclude that school officials should seriously consider the potential dangers that may be associated with assigning supervision of peer helping programs to anyone other than a master's level counselor or similarly trained mental health professional.

Paraprofessionals and
Other Noncertificated Personnel

Administrators often hire noncertificated staff to assist in guidance functions. These noncertificated personnel include career technicians and guidance secretaries. Enthusiastic and capable, often more visible to students on the "front line," paraprofessionals can be invaluable in enhancing the school climate while servicing daily needs in the career and guidance centers. As with graduate students, teacher advisors, and peer facilitators, effective use of paraprofessionals and other noncertificated personnel requires (a) clear job descriptions that identify what is and what is not within their scope of competence; (b) inservice training to understand their legal and ethical responsibilities, as well as their relationship to the overall school milieu; (c) and ongoing supervision by in-house school counselors to bridge their work with teachers, administrators, and parents who share in the student's mission for school success.

Conclusion

Administrators can effectively supplement guidance and counseling services through judicious use of school counseling graduate students, teacher advisors, peer facilitators, and paraprofessional, noncertificated personnel. Specific actions to take in order to avoid increased harm to students as well as ethical and legal violations include careful screening of the candidates and ongoing involvement with the school counselor(s) throughout the process. A well-trained, professional school counselor can provide supervision, consultation, and coordination for the many individuals involved in the comprehensive guidance program in working to achieve school goals.

References

American School Counselor Association. (1984.) *Ethical standards for school counselors.* (Adopted by ASCA Delegate Assembly March 19, 1984.)

California Commission on Teacher Credentialing. (1996.) *Information advisory on Education Code Section 49600 concerning teacher advisement programs.* (Draft.) Sacramento, CA.

Council for Accreditation of Counseling and Related Educational Programs. (1994.) *CACREP Accreditation Standards and Procedures Manual.* Alexandria, VA: American Counseling Association.

Lewis, M. W., & Lewis, A. C. (1996.) Peer helping programs: Helper role, supervisor training, and suicidal behavior. *Journal of Counseling & Development, 74,* 307-313.

John A. Casey is a counselor educator in the Department of Counseling and Educational Psychology at the University of Nevada, Reno, NV.

Penny Chennell is a superintendent with the Potter Valley Community Unified School District in rural northern Mendocino County, CA.

What a School Administrator Needs to Know About *Group Counseling*

Teesue H. Fields & David E. Losey

Group counseling can be one of the most effective, efficient ways for the school counselor to succeed with a wide variety of academic, social, and behavioral issues in K–12 schools. Administrators, teachers, and parents first need to understand the purpose of using group work and the expectations, benefits, and limitation of this counseling tool.

Reasons for Using Group Counseling

Group counseling allows school counselors to see six to eight students at one time, which increases counselor efficiency. However, the even more powerful reasons for using groups include: helping students learn from each other, letting students see models of positive behaviors, and allowing them to practice new behaviors in front of peers. Being in a group also allows the student to experience some of the universality of his or her problem: "I'm not the only one who has trouble with this!" (Corey & Corey, 1996)

There are primarily two kinds of groups used in schools. The guidance group focuses on students interested in a particular topic. Themes such as stress management, making friends, improving school success, dealing with loss, dealing with parental divorce and remarriage are common group topics in a comprehensive developmental guidance program. The school counselor may do a needs assessment of students, teachers, and parents to determine the groups most needed that year. Or the counselor may offer a group as a follow-up for a series of classroom guidance lessons, allowing struggling students to continue to practice new skills. The sessions in a guidance group are usually very structured with part of the session devoted to education on the topic and part of the session devoted to helping students apply the new knowledge to their own lives.

The other type of school group is a counseling group. This group consists of students with particular types of problems who meet to talk about and deal with their problems. A very common high school counseling group is an after-care group for students who have been in treatment for substance abuse. The recovering abusers need the support of students at school to stay clean and they need to find a new peer group who refuses to use drugs. Another common type of counseling group might be formed for students experiencing grief due to the unexpected death of a classmate. Group work allows students to deal with their grief and draw support from each other.

Selection for Group

It is crucial that students be screened by the leader before they are placed in a group. In fact, the ethical guidelines of both the Association for Specialists in Group Work (ASGW, 1989) and the American School Counselor Association (ASCA, 1994) state that students must have a screening interview before being placed in a group. The interview allows the school counselor to explain the purpose and general rules for a group, answer questions from the student, and assess the student's suitability for group. Some students have too many problems or are too disruptive or too shy to function effectively in a group. It is also important that the group contain a balance of types of students. It would be an absolute disaster to put eight acting-out, aggressive students in the same group. The group has to contain some students who can model positive behavior or students who have dealt with similar problems in the past and can explain their experience

(Smead, l995).

When students are interviewed for the group, the counselor explains that not everyone will be selected. The school counselor may want to offer a similar group the next semester and put the non-selected students at the top of the list. Or the counselor may need to offer individual counseling for students too problematic to be suitable for group.

Confidentiality

In the interview and at the first session, the school counselor explains that what happens in the group is confidential. If students talk about the group with those outside the group, then trust will be spoiled and the group will not function effectively. The counselor will also explain the exceptions to confidentiality, so that if students talk about harming themselves or someone else, or say they are being abused, the counselor will have to break confidentiality and report to the parents and the school and/or other authorities in order to keep the student safe.

Although principals and some parents may be concerned that things said in group will be talked about widely, there is ample evidence that students treat confidentiality very seriously and are protective of their group. Even though counselors cannot guarantee that no one in the group will break confidentiality, this breach of trust rarely happens.

Schools do a lot of classroom groups, such as reading groups, cooperative learning groups, and service learning groups. However, counseling groups are very different. There is no teacher or parent involvement in counseling groups and it is important that teachers and parents respect the confidentiality of the group process so that the group can be effective. However, parents and school staff should be assured that the school counselor will not probe students or push them to reveal information. The group leader tells students to disclose at their own level of comfort and to "pass" anytime they feel uncomfortable with a topic being discussed.

Parent Informed Consent

It is important that parents clearly understand the purpose of group and give informed consent for their child to be in the group. If the school counselor has done an effective job of publicizing the school guidance program, parents will already know that group counseling is one of the components of their school's program. The parent of a student chosen for group should receive a letter outlining the purpose of the group, a summary of topics to be covered in the group, and a review of the experience and credentials of the group leader. The letter can also cover the duration of the group and the plans for making up missed class time. A permission form should be attached for the parent's signature which might repeat some of the information about the group, with an additional statement that indicates the parent understands the need for confidentiality with the exceptions explained. When parents clearly understand the group process, they can provide the support necessary to make group a positive experience.

Logistics of Group Work

Groups usually consist of six to eight students. Groups larger than eight students do not permit all individuals an opportunity to work on their goals. School groups are usually time limited, but must meet for a minimum of eight to ten sessions to be effective. Guidance groups may meet for the minimum, while counseling groups may last an entire semester or occasionally an entire year. Sessions will last from 30–50 minutes in elementary school, depending on the age of the students. Secondary school groups usually last the entire class period.

Teachers need to be informed that a student will miss class for a counselor-led activity, but the teacher does not always need to know the reason for the group. It is important that students be given an opportunity to make up missed work and receive no penalty for missing class due to the group. Counselors and teachers need to work out an effective way to get passes to students and reminders to teachers that the student will miss class. It should be the responsibility of the counselor and student to carry out an effective schedule for group and a plan for making up missed work.

To lessen the time away from academics and minimize the disruption to a teacher's schedule, the group schedule can be handled in a variety of ways. In elementary school it might be possible to have group during a time that is usually not as heavy on instruction, such as the time before lunch or time at the end of the day. Or it may make more sense to rotate the time of group each week so that students don't miss the same subject.

In middle or high school, the group could meet a different period each week so that students don't miss the same class repeatedly. It might also be possible to use study hall time, if the selected students have the same schedule. In block scheduling, there is often a common research or tutoring period that could be used for group. Some schools have also included a thirty minute block that backs up to lunch and can be used for assemblies or special activities like group counseling or academic advising.

Group work is an essential part of a school's comprehensive developmental guidance program. If an administrator provides the encouragement and support for the school counselor to do groups in the school, then the counselor will have a powerful tool for successfully addressing the academic, social, and behavioral problems of students.

References

American School Counselor Association. (1994). *Ethical guidelines for school counselors*. Alexandria, VA: Author.

Association for Specialists in Group Work. (1989). *Ethical guidelines for group counselors*. Alexandria, VA: Author.

Corey, M. S., & Corey, G. (1996). *Groups: Process and practice*. Pacific Grove, CA: Brooks/Cole.

Smead, R. (1995). *Skills and techniques for group work with children and adolescents*. Champaign, IL: Research Press.

Teesue H. Fields is Assistant Professor of Counselor Education at Indiana University Southeast, New Albany, IN.

David E. Losey is Principal, Stout Elementary School, Sellersburg, IN.

Chapter 15

What a School Administrator Needs to Know About the School Counselor's Role With Families

Kenneth W. Simington & Ron J. Montaquila

Working with families has always been an integral component of the school counselor's work. A commitment to working with families is often tempered by the struggle to balance the need to assist families while attending to the other basic roles and services required by the school. As counselors seek to successfully negotiate the balance between school and family needs, the support of school administrators is critical.

Most would acknowledge that the primary task of school counselors is to assist students with achieving educational success, and although they are typically viewed as support services in the school setting, guidance and counseling services do contribute significantly to students' educational successes. From kindergarten to high school, counselors are routinely called upon by parents to provide information regarding accurate educational placements, assessment of academic skills and abilities, and skills related to school success.

The last several decades have seen unprecedented changes in the family. The prototypical family structure in American society, the nuclear family, has given way to a diversity of family structures. Popenoe (1990) noted that several factors have contributed to the changing family structure, including an ever-increasing divorce rate and an increased percentage of two-parent workers in families. Thus, school counselors are confronted with the challenge of providing meaningful and effective services for a wide variety of family structures. These structures include (a) single parent families; (b) families separated by divorce; and (c) families created by remarriage (i.e., blended or step-families). While all families are confronted with "universal" concerns and issues, each of the particular family structures presents unique and idiosyncratic difficulties that require much skill and expertise by the school counselor. Counselors can no longer operate under the concept of the normative family structure but must be resourceful and flexible in providing services to families in the school setting. As the institution of the family continues to change, school counselors must continue to update their skills so they will be able to assist these families. The remainder of this capsule outlines particular services provided by school counselors to assist families.

Counselor Services With Families

Family needs for school counseling vary greatly. Depending upon the needs of students and their families, the services provided can range from low intensity (e.g., information) to high intensity (e.g., counseling). Critical to the school counselor's effectiveness with students and their families is accurate assessment of their presenting needs and determination of the most appropriate service delivery model. The American School Counselor Association has identified three broad areas by which school counselors provide a range of services (ACES-ASCA, 1966). These three areas are (a) Counseling, (b) Consulting, and (c) Coordination. Within these three broad areas, counselors provide a continuum of services.

Counseling

Counseling services are at the very core of services provided by school counselors. Parents and families of the 1990s find that the counseling services of school counselors are helpful in many situations. From elementary school to high school, school counselors have welcomed requests from parents to assist their little Johnny or Susie. With regards to counseling services, many parents are encouraged to pursue these services on the basis of previously established working relationships between their child and the counselor.

Counselors have long recognized that while working with students, either individually or in groups, the work ultimately being done involves and impacts families. With the rapidly changing nature of families in recent years, interest in counseling services for families in the school setting has increased tremendously. As schools have encouraged greater participation by parents in the education of their children, school counselors have been involving parents more intensively in counseling services. Although not typically thought of as a service by school counselors, brief family counseling in the right context and setting, has increasing appeal. School counselors have recognized the positive impact of limited brief family counseling services in the school and are being trained to provide this service as a part of their comprehensive guidance programs (Hinkle & Wells, 1995).

Consulting

School counselors have also assisted families by providing indirect services in the form of consultation. Indirect services are provided to the student where there is no direct contact between the counselor and the student. Parents often seek guidance from school counselors regarding age appropriate and developmental concerns. One ASCA (1980) role statement acknowledged that school counselors must "accommodate parents who need assistance with understanding normal child growth and development; improving family communication skills; or understanding their role in encouraging children to learn."

During each level of their school experience, parental anxiety and concerns for children abound. For the child in the elementary school, parents may be concerned about the overall adjustment of their child in the school environment. This concern about adjustment focuses not only on students' academic well-being, but their psychological, behavioral, and social adjustment as well. The parent and family of a middle or junior high school student comes face to face with the "storm and stress" of adolescence. Many parents seek the latest in information and research regarding adolescent development. School counselors are appropriately trained to provide the necessary expertise for parents during this critical developmental period. When students enter high school and parents' attention turns toward life after high school, school counselors provide fundamental services to help students reach their life and career goals. Parents expect counselors to know more than what are the "good" or "hot" colleges, but which of these colleges is best for their child. During the high school years, adolescents in this middle stage are confronted with the big four of adolescent problems: (a) sex, (b) drugs, (c) depression, and (d) violence (Dryfoos, 1990). Adolescents who are solidly in the identity stage of development may leave bewildered parents in the dark about most aspects of their lives. In conjunction with this factor, the adolescent during this period actively seeks out the advice, counsel, and approval of peers in developing this sense of identity. Certainly what school counselors have to offer in this regard can be extremely helpful to parents.

Coordinating

Myrick (1993) defined coordination as "the process of managing different indirect guidance services to students, including special events and general procedures" (p. 297). Through coordination services, school counselors are able to assist families with information and appropriate community referrals to qualified professionals for educational and mental health related services. Schmidt (1996) noted that school counselors are the appropriate school personnel to provide referral services given that "counselors are familiar with the breadth of community services, they design assessment techniques to gather initial data for referrals, and as members of a helping profession, they establish effective communication with service providers outside the school" (p. 111). Many families find that the referral services provided by counselors are central to the resolution of developing or existing crises with their children. A related and equally important service is that of follow-up. Follow-up may be necessary where there are school implications. With positive relationships established, counselors can serve as the communication link between the family and school when circumstances warrant.

Conclusion

The school counselor's work with families is in a state of transition as we head into the 21st century. As families have changed, so has the school counselor's role in assisting these families. In recent years, counselors have begun to expand their base of services to provide additional services not historically provided by school counselors. School counselors stand willing and able to deliver effective and comprehensive developmental guidance and counseling programs. With the continued support of school administrators, providing an array of services to meet the needs of students and their families will continue to be an important part of that effort.

References

American School Counselor Association. (1990). ASCA defines the role of the school counselor. *The ASCA Counselor, 28,* 10.

Association for Counselor Education and Supervision-American School Counselor Association. (1966). *Report of the ACES-ASCA joint committee on the elementary school counselor.* Washington, DC: ACA Press.

Dryfoos, J. H. (1990). *Adolescents at risk: Prevalence and prevention.* New York: Oxford University Press.

Hinkle, J. S., & Wells, M. E. (1995). *Family counseling in the schools: Practical strategies for counselors, teachers, and psychologists.* Greensboro, NC: ERIC/CASS.

Myrick, R. D. (1993). *Developmental guidance and counseling: A practical approach* (2nd ed.). Minneapolis, MN: Educational Media.

Popenoe, D. (1990). Family decline in America. In D. G. Blankenhorn, S. Bayne, & J. B. Elshtain (Eds.), *Rebuilding the nest: A new commitment to the American family* (pp. 3-25). Milwaukee, WI: Family Service America.

Schmidt, J. J. (1996). *Counseling in schools: Essential services and comprehensive programs.* Boston: Allyn and Bacon.

Kenneth W. Simington, Ph.D., is Assistant Professor of Human Services, University of Virginia, Charlottesville, VA.

Ron J. Montaquila, Ed.D., is Assistant Superintendent, Winston-Salem/Forsyth County Schools, Winston-Salem, NC.

Chapter 16

What a School Administrator Needs to Know About *Expressive Arts and Play Media in School Counseling*

Pamela O. Paisley & Robert E. Young III

School counselors provide a number of direct counseling interventions to children and adolescents including individual counseling, small groups, and classroom guidance. Although school counselors are primarily employed to support the educational process, oftentimes personal or social issues arise which interfere with student learning. Counseling sessions, either individually or in groups, can alleviate or ameliorate such concerns and allow the student's focus to return to the important tasks of the classroom. Counseling can also support the affective and interpersonal development of the child or adolescent. To facilitate these processes, play media and expressive arts are sometimes used in providing school counseling services, particularly to children.

Rationale

At first glance, these creative interventions may appear to be "too much fun," frivolous, or without clear purpose to an observer. It is important, however, to look beyond the surface to determine the rationale for these approaches. Unlike adults, whose primary method of communication is through verbalization, children do not have the vocabulary or experience to conceptualize issues or problems (Landreth, 1991). Creative approaches can provide an alternative method for communication. Sometimes, even in working with adolescents and adults, expressive arts can offer a way to overcome cognitive defenses. As an example, a trauma at a particular stage of development may have presented a psychological block that an adolescent will need to overcome in order to be fully functioning or to fulfill his or her potential.

To summarize the best rationale for using play media and expressive arts in working with school-aged children, we can say that

- With children, it provides the most developmentally appropriate intervention.
- With adolescents, it may be the most appropriate intervention or it may provide a method for overcoming developmental blocks or obstacles.
- This approach does provide a window into the child's world. A child may not be able to *tell* us what is wrong but may be able to *show* us *if we pay attention.*
- This approach provides an opportunity to promote development and empower the child or adolescent.

Theoretical Foundations

Play therapy or the use of creative arts in any type of therapy can be approached using numerous theoretical foundations. Individual clinicians and researchers have provided in-depth information, resources, and insights based on particular orientations. Melanie Klein and Anna Freud are associated with psychoanalytic approaches; Clark Moustakas with existential; Virginia Axline, Garry Landreth, and Louise and Bernard Guerney with child-centered; Terry Kottman with Adlerian; Violet Oaklander with Gestalt; and John Allan with Jungian. The particular orientation will affect the amount of direction given, the strategies chosen, and the amount of interpretation provided.

Regardless of approach, however, most play therapists or counselors who use expressive arts in their work with children usually agree on certain points:

    1. Children usually do not have the verbal skills to ask for help in order to work through their problems.

106

Play provides one of the best ways to communicate with children and "see their world."

2. Expressive arts and play media are seen as methods to help children express their feelings, explore real- life situations, test limits, and develop a positive sense of self and others.

3. Relationship-building strategies are used such as tracking behavior, restatement of content, and clarification of feelings.

4. Some types of behaviors must be limited.

Types of Media

School counselors use a wide variety of media to facilitate relationship-building, to provide information in assessment, and to generally be used in the working stages of therapeutic change. Gladding (1992) notes the range in counseling interventions using music, dance/movement, imagery, visual arts, literature, creative writing, drama, play, and humor. He suggests that in using any of these media, the arts provide an experience that is "process-oriented, emotionally-sensitive, socially directed, and awareness-focused" and that enable "people from diverse backgrounds to develop in ways that are personally enhancing and enjoyable." (p. ix).

Most often in schools, counselors tend to use visual arts, clay, journalling, children's literature, and toys. Visual arts include a range within its own parameters including crayons, markers, water colors, finger paints, and various forms of collage. Clay is also used in several forms including the familiar play-dough, as well as the more versatile and artistic media associated with plasticene and earthen clay. Each has advantages depending upon the purpose of the activity. Journalling is often used in small groups as a way of counselors staying abreast of individual issues for participants while allowing students another avenue for self-expression.

Bibliotherapy is also used in the counseling process related to particular issues for individual children (e.g., a child experiencing a death in the family is given a book centered on that theme). In addition, children's literature, when selected using appropriate guidelines for quality, can also be used as a classroom guidance intervention to assist in promoting cognitive and interpersonal development, as well as providing a bonding experience for students (Borders & Paisley, 1993). Borders and Naylor (1994) authors of *Children Talking About Books* have provided a significant resource for teachers and counselors related to the use of quality children's literature.

Toys are also often used, especially by elementary school counselors. Landreth (1991) suggests certain criteria for selection of toys for a counselor's office, including selecting toys which provide (a) facilitation of a wide range of creative and emotional expression; (b) engagement of children's interests, exploration, and expression without verbalization; (c) opportunities for success without defined structure or commitment; and (d) sturdiness in their construction. Landreth also encourages counselors to have toys available from three broad categories of toys including *real-life toys* (e.g., doll house, doll family), *acting-out/aggressive-release toys* (e.g., bop bag, alligator puppet, rubber knife), and *toys for creative expression and emotional release* (e.g., sand, water).

Research Results

A summary of the results of play therapy research studies (Landreth, 1991) indicate that effectiveness has been demonstrated in numerous settings and in various problem areas. Effectiveness studies were conducted in settings such as hospitals and psychiatric settings as well as in schools. Effected problem areas ranged from specific behaviors such as hair pulling to general emotional adjustment of children affected by divorce or abuse. Certain physical or psychosomatic conditions have also been improved (e.g., asthma, colitis, allergies, stuttering) using play therapy. The only diagnostic categories not identified as benefiting from these types of interventions involve autism and extreme cases of schizophrenia. Perhaps, most significant for school counselors– based on the populations with whom they work and the basic assumptions for school counseling programs– are the significant results that have been found in the following areas: (a) improved reading performance; (b) increased academic performance for students with learning disabilities; (c) better social and emotional adjustment; (d) improved self-concept; (e) decreased aggressive, acting-out behaviors; and (f) stress and anxiety reduction.

Conclusion

Expressive arts and play media provide an important tool for school counselors in providing services to children and adolescents. These approaches offer an alternative method of communication or as what Violet Oaklander (1988) describes as a *window to our children*. Creative techniques can reduce problem behaviors, increase desired outcomes, and generally promote healthy cognitive, affective, and interpersonal development.

References

Borders, S. G., & Naylor, A. P. (1994). *Children talking about books*. Phoenix: Oryx.

Borders, S. G., & Paisley, P. O. (1993). Children's literature as a resource for classroom guidance. *Elementary School Guidance and Counseling, 27,* 131-139.

Gladding, S. T. (1992). *Counseling as an art: The creative arts in counseling*. Alexandria, VA: American Association for Counseling and Development.

Landreth, G. L. (1991). *Play therapy: The art of the relationship*. Muncie, IN: Accelerated Development.

Additional Resources for Counselors and Administrators

Allan, J. (1988). *Inscapes of the child's world*. Dallas: Spring Publications.

Kottman, T. (1995). *Partners in play: An Adlerian approach to play therapy*. Alexandria, VA: American Counseling Association.

Landreth, G. L. (1990). *Play therapy bibliography*. Denton, TX: Center for Play Therapy.

Moustakas, C. E. (1992). *Psychotherapy with children: The living relationship*. Greeley, CO: Carron.

Oaklander, V. (1988). *Windows to our children*. Highland, NY: Center for Gestalt Development.

Thompson, A. L., & Rudolph, L. B. (1992). *Counseling children*. Pacific Grove, CA: Brooks/Cole.

Pamela O. Paisley, Ed.D., NCC is Associate Professor and School Counseling Program Coordinator, Department of Counseling and Human Development Services, University of Georgia, Athens, GA.

Robert E. Young III, M.S. is a retired elementary school principal and current headmaster at Avalon Academy, Dillon, SC.

Chapter 17

What a School Administrator Needs to Know About the School Counselor's Role With Teenage Parents

Mark S. Kiselica & Howard Colvin

Teenage pregnancy and parenthood is one of the major social issues confronting school professionals in the United States. Each year about one million adolescent girls become pregnant, about a half million adolescent girls give birth to a child (U.S. Bureau of the Census, 1996), and the majority of these births occur out of wedlock (Bachu, 1995). Consequently, a substantial number of adolescents face parenthood during their school-age years.

The many challenges associated with adolescent parenthood—learning parenting skills, arranging for adequate child care, managing financial difficulties, providing health care for the parents and the baby, addressing the strain placed on the immediate and extended family, juggling the responsibilities of being a parent and a student—place teenage mothers and fathers at-risk to drop out of school. In order to prevent young parents from leaving school prematurely, school systems can assist school-age parents with the transition to parenthood through the development and provision of a wide-range of services, including the following: child care; individual, couples, and family counseling; educational, career, and school-to-work transition counseling; instruction in parenting skills, financial planning, and health education; and health care for the adolescent parents and their children (Kiselica & Pfaller, 1993).

Typically, school-based, full-service programs for pregnant and parenting teenagers are organized through collaborative ventures between schools and local social service agencies and health organizations. Essential features of such programs include infant care and a special school curriculum, which allow teenage parents to continue with an education and to participate in work/ study cooperative programs (Flood, Greenspan, & Mundorf, 1985).

School counselors can play a central part in the organization and delivery of school-based programs for adolescent parents. This capsule describes for school administrators school counselor's role in school-wide efforts to assist young parents in completing their educations and in increasing their chances of becoming economically self-sufficient, responsible, and competent adults.

Outreach Counseling

Outreach counseling with teenage parents is essential for two reasons. First, many adolescent parents, particularly teenage fathers, are uncomfortable approaching school personnel about issues pertaining to their sexuality and an unplanned pregnancy. Second, unplanned pregnancies typically precipitate a period of crisis and acute confusion for the teenagers involved. Unless school counselors establish and practice outreach strategies for identifying pregnant and parenting students and engage them in counseling, many students may make rash and self-defeating decisions about how to resolve the pregnancy and whether or not they should remain in school (Kiselica & Murphy, 1994; Kiselica & Pfaller, 1993).

School counselors can employ a variety of tactics to identify students facing the dilemma of a crisis pregnancy. Many young, expectant parents can be identified through the utilization of formal referral networks that include the school nurse, teachers, administrators, parents, clergy, and health care professionals employed in local obstetrical-gynecological, pediatric, and planned parenthood clinics. Adolescent expectant parents can also be specified through the informal contacts developed between school counselors and students (Kiselica & Pfaller, 1993).

After the names of expectant student parents have surfaced, the school counselor faces the delicate and tricky task of engaging the young parents in counseling. The school counselor must somehow allay any fears the students have about counseling and convince the students that counseling will benefit them. To accomplish these tasks, the school counselor can provide crucial emotional support by empathizing with the students' dilemma and by addressing the young parents' most pressing need, such as directing them to health and child care services. Throughout this process the counselor must communicate to the students that he or she is the students' advocate who will support them until they have successfully weathered the storm created by the unplanned pregnancy. When these steps are taken, the students are likely to trust the counselor to guide them as they attempt to address a variety of educational, career, and personal concerns (Kiselica, 1995; Kiselica & Pfaller, 1993).

Educational, Career, and School-To-Work Transition Counseling

Educational, career, and school-to-work counseling with teenage parents varies according to the particular phase of pregnancy. During the prenatal phase, counseling involves crisis-oriented decision-making, much of which is centered around the dilemma of whether or not to drop out of school. Counseling during the postnatal phase includes long-term educational and career planning (Kiselica & Murphy, 1994; Kiselica & Pfaller, 1993).

During the prenatal counseling phase, the availability of multifaceted, school-based services—especially the provision of on-site child care—prevents many teenage parents, especially pregnant teenagers and adolescent mothers, from dropping out of school. The counselor's role in these schools is to educate the young parents about what services are available and how to use those services to manage the demands of school and parenthood. In schools lacking teenage parenting programs, the school counselor must work urgently with the teenage parents to settle child care arrangements for the baby and then ascertain if additional services, such as individual and family counseling, are necessary to help the students to complete their educations (Kiselica, 1995; Kiselica & Pfaller, 1993).

During the postnatal counseling phase, the school counselor can shift his or her attention to helping the teenage parents to develop realistic, long-term career plans. The school counselor should conduct career and self-exploration exercises, such as an orientation to the world of work and the completion of career interest inventories, which can help the clients to select a fulfilling career path. The school counselor also must lead the young parents in skills-building activities, such as filing work applications, writing resumes and work-related cover letters, and practicing interviewing and image-management skills, all of which can help the parents with the transition from school to work (Kiselica, 1995; Kiselica & Murphy, 1994).

Personal Counseling

Despite their best efforts to complete their educations and prepare for the work world, a variety of personal issues can jeopardize the young parents' ability to cope with their responsibilities. For example, they may feel overwhelmed at times with the challenge of learning how to be an effective parent or with the financial burdens associated with parenthood. In addition, conflicts between the teenage mother and father or between one or both of the adolescent parents and their extended families can cause considerable strain. Students struggling with these issues often turn to the school counselors for drop-in counseling through which the counselor can provide crucial emotional support and assess if the student requires additional services, such as couples and family counseling and training in financial-, time-, and stress-management skills (Kiselica, 1995).

Referral Services

Most school counselors will be hard pressed to directly provide the full range of services that adolescent parents commonly require. This is especially so for counselors employed in schools that do not house multifaceted teenage parent programs. Therefore, much of the school counselor's energy must be focused on developing and utilizing a referral network through which a variety of professionals assist the young parents with the transition to parenthood. In effect, the school counselor must become a broker of services who supportively guides the teenage parent through the social and health services systems. By working in this manner, the school counselor provides the young parent with reassurance and a sense of continuity as he or she attempts to navigate services provided outside of the school setting (Kiselica, 1995; Kiselica & Pfaller, 1993).

Conclusion

In the United States educational system there is a long-standing philosophical tradition of responding to the needs of the whole child in order to educate each child adequately and prepare them for the challenges of life (see Kiselica, 1995). When it comes to meeting the needs of adolescent parents who are students, school administrators face the difficult choice as to whether their schools will become a central base for a seamless web of services or a conduit to services available in the community at large. In either case, it is critical that schools contribute to a societal effort to help teenage parents. The research literature indicates that the provision of holistic service programs helps pregnant or parenting teenagers to become competent parents, and enables them to complete school, obtain employment, and avoid welfare dependency (Kiselica, 1995). Consequently, school administrators are urged to support school counselors as they provide direct and indirect services that will assist teenage parents with the transition to parenthood.

References

Bachu, A. (1995). Fertility among American women: June, 1994. *Current Population Reports, Series P-20, No. 482.*

Flood, M. F., Greenspan, S., & Mundorf, N. K. (1985). School-based services for pregnant and parenting adolescents. *Special Services in the Schools, 2,* 27-44.

Kiselica, M. S. (1995). *Multicultural counseling with teenage fathers: A practical guide.* Newbury Park, CA: Sage.

Kiselica, M. S., & Murphy, D. K. (1994). Developmental career counseling with teenage parents. *Career Development Quarterly, 42,* 238-244.

Kiselica, M. S., & Pfaller, J. (1993). Helping teenage parents: The independent and collaborative roles of school counselors and counselor educators. *Journal of Counseling and Development, 72,* 42-48.

U. S. Bureau of the Census. (1996). *Statistical abstract of the United States, 1996.* Washington DC: Author.

Mark S. Kiselica is Assistant Professor and Coordinator of the CACREP-accredited program in school counseling in the Department of Counseling and Personnel Services at the College of New Jersey, Trenton, NJ.

Howard Colvin is principal of the P. J. Hill Elementary School in Trenton, NJ.

Mark Kiselica and Howard Colvin are members of the Professional Development School Network of the School of Education of the College of New Jersey.

What a School Administrator Needs to Know About the School Counselor's Role With Special Education

Jackie M. Allen & Evelyn LaTorre

With the advent of the Education for All Handicapped Children Act (Public Law 94-142) in 1975 and the updating of that legislation with the Individuals with Disabilities Act (IDEA) in 1990, services for students with special needs have come to the attention of all educators. Yet in many schools there continues to be a lack of understanding of the real needs of many special education students, how to meet those needs programmatically, and who will deliver the services to meet those needs.

Some school counselor training programs do not require a course on any aspect of special education; therefore, some school counselors are not familiar with the special education process and are unaware of the needs of special students. Also, some special educators do not fully utilize all aspects of a school counseling program. Thus, school counselors do not serve special needs students to the fullest extent of program and service capacity.

The school counselor as a service provider for special education students is both an integral part of a comprehensive counseling and guidance program and an important member of an integrated services team. School programs for all students (pre–K through post-secondary) focus on the facilitation of student development and student learning. The American School Counselor Association has established school counseling program standards in academic development, career development, and personal and social development so that "counseling programs help ensure equal opportunity for all students to participate fully in the educational process" (1997). School counselors should actively serve all students, including special needs students, in their schools.

The Special Education Process

School counselors interface with the special education process in many ways. One major responsibility of all educators is to identify and serve at-risk students. Identification may occur through the Search and Serve process where a school counselor will make a referral for review and program modification for a specific student. The school counselor may serve as an important member of the Student Study Team that coordinates the at-risk referrals in a local school. Other appropriate school counselor functions may include: making referrals to the School Study Team, coordinating referrals, making observations, collecting background information, direct counseling, consulting on social/emotional development, making suggestions for program modification, direct behavior modification interventions, and consulting on placement recommendations. The school counselor, as student advocate, works as the school-based member of an integrated pupil personnel services team to effectively meet the academic, career, and social and personal developmental needs of all students.

Academic Development

One primary role of the school counselor in the local school is to facilitate academic school success for each student. Identification of at-risk students, including special needs students, is a primary responsibility. Providing academic guidance and counseling for appropriate class placement of each student is part of academic counseling. Becoming part of a 504 team to plan appropriate modifications for students with special needs is an important counseling role. Consultation with parents, teachers, and administrators is essential to ascertain the specific needs and to arrange for accommodation of those needs. Counselors help classroom teachers to provide a supportive learning environment for exceptional children through the modification of curriculum and homework, seating arrangements, student acceptance and inclusion in group work, and promotion of class participation. The school counselor as student advocate needs to champion the needs of the special student in program planning and evaluation, facilities development, and student activities. Developing strategies to help teachers work effectively with the parents of handicapped children and starting counseling groups for the parents are other important contributions the counselor can make. The goal should always be inclusion of the special needs student in all academic programming and placement.

Career Development

Whatever the handicapping situation, special needs students must be encouraged to develop their full potential. Career development, as part of a comprehensive counseling and guidance program, would be an area of emphasis for special needs students. The essential elements of career development are career awareness, career exploration, and career planning. In each phase of career development the special needs student requires not only special encouragement but specialized information. Career awareness for the special needs student must not be limited in scope since technology continues to provide ways for handicapped individuals to work at a variety of occupations not thought possible 20 years ago. Career exploration should include information about specialized training programs, colleges with programs for learning disabled students, regional center programs, and other programs available through federal, state, and private funds. Experiencing the world of work through service opportunities and work experience must be included in career exploration. Through the special education process of Transition Plans each student should be doing career planning that includes realistic and challenging goals and positive career experiences so that transition from school to work becomes a reality for each special needs student. School counselors, as student advocates, can teach students to become self advocates, learning how to best present themselves as individuals with special talents and abilities to contribute to the work force.

Social/Personal Development

Perhaps one of the most difficult areas for special needs students is in their social and personal development. Both parents and students need special assistance in understanding the nature of the disability and how to deal on a personal and emotional level with the challenges presented by that disability. Thus, it is critical that school counselors work with parents, teachers, and students to ensure that all are well informed about (a) the nature of the student's disability; (b) the ramifications in regards to learning, socialization, and personal development; and (c) the ways in which students can be assisted to adjust to the school environment. To accomplish this work, school counselors need to (a) be informed about an individual student's diagnosis (e.g., attention deficit disorder); (b) understand psychoeducational reports, including Diagnostic and Statistical Manual of Disorders IV terminology; and (c) comprehend Individual Education Plans (IEP). Classroom guidance units on problem-solving, conflict resolution, peer relationships, family relationships, and self-esteem are important for special needs students. Another area in which the school counselor can be very effective is in the development of behavior management plans. Counselors contribute through classroom observations, a review of student records, understanding the individual needs of the student and the curriculum, and participation in the development of the behavior management plan. Parents of special education students have special needs that often can best be served through family counseling and parent education. Special counseling groups for these parents will help them work through their grief over the student's disability, improve interpersonal relationships with their student and their student's teachers, understand their rights, learn how to advocate effectively for their student's benefit, and become more involved in the education process. Counselors, in consultation with school psychologists or other integrated services team members, will make referrals to community agencies when appropriate.

Conclusion

What must school counselors know to be more effective in meeting the needs of special education students? First, if counselors have not already had a class in special education law and procedures, they should take such a class or educate themselves by borrowing special education materials from colleagues or surfing the Internet for pertinent information. Counselors need to understand mainstreaming concepts, the identification process, the development of individual education plans, student and parents rights, and how to develop behavioral plans and 504 modifications. In addition, a thorough knowledge in the interpretation of psychoeducational reports, test data, and the characteristics of common disorders will prove useful in working with parents and staff to understand the nature of student disabilities, special needs, and placement.

Many school counselors are already providing excellent services for special needs students through comprehensive counseling and guidance programs. Other school counselors are collaborating with school nurses, school psychologists, and school social workers through integrated services teams to effectively meet the needs of special students. With some additional information and inservice training all school counselors can help teachers in (a) modifying curriculum; (b) working with special students to maximize their potential; (c) making appropriate counseling interventions with special education students and their parents; and (d) being an informed advocate for special needs students. Special needs students will then be served equally when all their unique needs are met.

References

American School Counselor Association. (1997). *National standards for school counseling programs.* Draft of unpublished manuscript.

Gerler, E. (1991). *The changing world of the elementary school counselor* (Report No. EDO-CG-90-3). Ann Arbor, MI: ERIC Clearinghouse on Counseling and Personnel Services. (ERIC Document Reproduction Service No. ED 328 824).

Idol, L., & Baran, S. (1992). Elementary school counselors and special educators consulting together: Perilous pitfalls or opportunities to collaborate? *Elementary School Guidance and Counseling 26*, 202-213.

West, B. L. (1992). *School counselor preparation towards working with students with disabilities* (Report No. CG024351). Seminar Paper, Ohio University.(ERIC Document Reproduction Service No. No. ED 347 423)

Dr. Jackie M. Allen is a past president of ASCA, has been a junior high and high school counselor and a school psychologist in the Fremont Unified School District for 25 years and is an adjunct instructor at Chapman University, Los Angles, CA.

Dr. Evelyn LaTorre is Program Administrator II, in Far East County Contra Costa County Office of Special Education. She has been the Director of Special Education in San Jose Unified School District, San Jose, CA.

Chapter 19

What a School Administrator Needs to Know About the School Counselor's Role With Multicultural Student Populations

Darlene Sellers & Tonya Hall

Working with multicultural student populations goes deeper than organizing activities for "National Black History Month" and decorating bulletin boards that recognize St. Patrick's Day or Chinese New Year. This is not to say that celebrations of ethnic, race, religion, and national origin differences are not important. However, school counselors recognize that multicultural student populations present to school administrators and teachers unique developmental perspectives and personal concerns different from those we have served in the past. Most important, when school culture reflects the unifying nature of inclusion and acceptance, while at the same time celebrating and appreciating each individual's uniqueness and value, internalized societal stereotypes and negative self and own-group concepts are overcome.

With *Brown v. the Board of Education* in 1954, schools were mandated to provide educational equity to a wide range of groups, such as females, disabled persons, and ethnic groups. Furthermore, schools were charged with providing students environments that were integrated, pluralistic, equal-opportunity-oriented, and democratic. In the past, most school counselors focused their attention on promoting equal opportunity for students in academics and career decision-making. Today, additional roles played by school counselors include helping students develop multicultural competencies and skills in order to cope with issues they are facing, or likely to face, in our contemporary society.

Increasing multicultural competencies is not limited to individual intervention; it involves the school community. A mandate for school counselors is to promote appreciation for the "worth, dignity, potential, and uniqueness of each individual" (American Counseling Association, 1995). Hand-in-hand with this position are intervention strategies planned with culturally diverse populations in mind. The primary goal of schools is to help students graduate; thus, most interventions are aimed at keeping multicultural students in school, providing opportunities for them to experience academic success, develop friendships, and maintain healthy relationships with others.

School counselors know how important it is to explore the benefits and costs of group identification, including positive and negative consequences. In addition, opportunities are orchestrated to help students experience and appreciate what it means to be a part of any group and how to make informed choices. Notwithstanding interventions with students, developing multicultural competency is viewed as a school-wide responsibility. Through the discussion that follows, a brief description of intervention strategies that target multicultural student populations is presented.

Group counseling. Group counseling services and group guidance programs help students develop essential skills. Group processes may specifically focus on self-esteem, career goals, relationship skills, study and test-taking skills, or problem-solving skills. Group experiences build skills and help students learn how they are unique as individuals, yet share in common interests and concerns. Small group counseling provides more individual attention and follow-up than large group guidance activities and meets students' needs for building healthy identity development.

Individual counseling. There are times when students need more individualized attention. Individual counseling requires an accurate assessment of a student's present situation and level of functioning. This means careful consideration of socioeconomic and cultural biases that may be present in assessments instruments and processes.

School counselors recognize the importance of fully and openly exploring the possibilities and consequences of behavior change in relationship to students' cultural diversity. Literature relating to individual and group counseling interventions with culturally diverse students places strong emphasis on the development of self-esteem and individual worth. With the exception of destructive, disruptive, and violent behaviors, school counselors carefully consider any treatment plans with goals that alter behaviors.

Faculty support. Teachers have significant influence on the development and education of children. Yet, many teachers work in schools with cultural and social influences that are much different from their own backgrounds. There are times when these teachers experience uncertainty and find themselves in complex situations. School counselors can provide resources, support, and intervention plans when cultural differences between teachers and students jeopardize the teaching and learning environment. Equally important is encouraging teachers to set high expectations for students. However, we emphasize that accurate assessments and reasonable expectations help guard against biased perceptions of cultural differences.

Family services. Providing services that are responsive to the changing needs of students and their families demands more attention today than in the past. In many cases, family structures are mixtures of relationships, unions, and groups that make it difficult to define exactly what we mean by home and family. The school counselor learns about families by interviewing children, reading cumulative records, visiting the homes of students, and assessing the needs of families. Assisting families in obtaining needed social services, conferencing with parents and guardians, and developing communication "links" between the school and home, all these efforts build alliances with students' families that may assist in student retention.

Program evaluation. Developing needs assessments and outcome evaluation plans that inform us about the effectiveness of counseling programs and school interventions are becoming more important. Increasing numbers of our youth are growing up in circumstances that limit their chances for successful lives. More and more children–especially those who are poor and those who must deal with discrimination–are facing everyday experiences that fail to provide the resources, supports, and opportunities essential for healthy development and reasonable preparation for productive adult lives (National Research Council, 1993). Thus, an important component of effective and efficient program development and planning involves evaluation.

Community awareness. An important role for school counselors is to become informed about the community, customs, traditions, and values that interact with the mission of the school. This is accomplished through meeting people, touring the community, joining civic organizations, and observing and participating in community events.

Orchestrating school culture. Cultural beliefs and traditions established in the home are often devalued in the school setting (Cole, Thomas, & Lee, 1988). Thus, characteristics defining school culture need to be carefully designed to empower the entire population. School counselors can provide developmental perspectives when creating mission statements that assist in promoting respect and acceptance of human diversity.

Professional development. The *Ethical Standards for School Counselors* "recognizes that differences in clients relating to age, gender, race, religion, sexual orientation, socioeconomic and ethnic background may require specific training to ensure competent services" (American School Counselor Association, 1994, p. 3). We increase our multicultural competency by participating in continuing education opportunities, professional conferences, and training. An important professional responsibility is designing opportunities to share this information with teachers, administrators, parents, and community members.

While not explicitly expressed, this discussion implies that contextual conditions unique to a particular school's multicultural student population may play a part in influencing what intervention strategies are implemented. In summary, counselors play key roles with administrators and teachers in schools that (a) provide training in multicultural competencies; (b) encourage sensitivity to individual differences and understanding of oneself andothers; (c) provide knowledge and skills necessary to work with special populations. Additionally, school counselors respond proactively to prejudicial attitudes and values that influence assessment and treatment with multicultural students. Direct intervention strategies are provided to students and families. Thus, school counselors assume an active role in creating a school culture that empowers all individuals to succeed and reach their fullest potential.

References

American Counseling Association. (1995). *ACA code of ethics and standards of practice.* Alexandria, VA: Author.

American School Counselor Association. (1994). *American School Counselor Association ethical standards for school counselors.* Alexandria, VA: Author.

Cole, S. M., Thomas, A. R., & Lee, C. C. (1988). School counselor and school psychologists: Partners in minority family outreach. *Journal of Multicultural Counseling and Development, 16,* 110-116.

National Research Council. (1993). *Losing generations.* Washington, D.C.: National Academy Press.

Darlene Sellers, Ph.D., is Assistant Professor of Psychology and Coordinator of the School Counseling Program, Division of Education and Psychology, University of Southern Mississippi Gulf Coast, Long Beach, MS.

Tonya Hall, M.Ed., is Principal of Gaston Point Elementary School, Gulfport, MS.

What a School Administrator Needs to Know About School Counseling Professionalism: Ethics, Clinical Supervision, and Professional Associations

Lori B. Crutchfield & Elizabeth S. Hipps

School principals recognize the essential nature of the continuing professional development of the professionals on their staffs. School counselors have unique needs that are not addressed through traditional staff development activities planned for other professionals,—meeting those needs must be included in administrative plans for professional development. Counselors should make their unique needs known to their administrators, and principals need to be open to requests for support for such content-specific activities. We wrote this capsule in hopes that administrators, upon reading it, would have a better idea of what their school counselors should be doing in order to maintain an appropriate level of professionalism.

In the following pages, professional issues salient to school counselors and administrators will be discussed. This list is not all-inclusive, but three broad categories (ethics, clinical supervision, and professional associations) are addressed. The issue of school counseling professionalism suffers from limited exposure within the educational administration field, and it is hoped that this document will encourage a productive professional dialogue on the topic.

Ethics

Professional school counselors are bound by the ethical standards of both the American Counseling Association [ACA] (1995) and the American School Counselor Association [ASCA] (1992). These standards provide guidelines in numerous professional areas, including client (student) confidentiality and parents' rights. One area that is often difficult to navigate within schools is the issue of minor students' rights to confidentiality. School counselors are ethically bound to respect the wishes of their minor clients regarding the confidentiality of private issues they have discussed. This often leads to misunderstandings between counselors and faculty over access to such information. When, for example, teachers request the details of a session with their students, the administrator should support the counselor's request to maintain confidentiality. Although no ethical standard for administrators addresses the issue directly, ethical codes do support the protection of the confidentiality rights of students. The code of ethics developed by the American Association of School Administrators [AASA](1976) and adopted by the National Association of Elementary School Principals and the National Association of Secondary School Principals includes a standard requiring that the administrator make "the well-being of students the fundamental value of all decision making and actions" (p. 12).

Because most clients in the school setting are minors, counselors' ethical and legal obligations sometimes differ. For example, if a 12-year-old student divulges sensitive information to the counselor regarding behaviors with friends and that child's parent demands access to this disclosure, legally that parent has a right to the information. Ethically, however, the student should give permission before any confidential information is discussed with a third party. For many counselors, this raises a serious dilemma. Legal and ethical experts clearly state that a code of ethics may not require someone to break a law. Thus, both counselors and administrators should bend to legal obligations first. Of course, this can be done in an ethical manner. In the above situation, the counselor might encourage the student to share the information with his or her parent, or get the parent to seek the child's permission to hear the information.

Clinical Supervision

Professional development for school counselors can take many forms. Workshops and independent readings add important knowledge and skills to a professional school counselor's repertoire. Supervision also plays a pivotal role in a counselor's personal and professional development. It is generally agreed that there are three types of supervision for school counselors (Roberts & Borders, 1994). The first, and most readily available, is administrative supervision. This is usually provided by the building principal or other administrator, and is focused on compliance with school requirements and accountability. The second type of supervision for school counselors is program supervision, generally provided by the designated central office counselor supervisor. The focus of this type of supervision is on the coordination and implementation of the overall school counseling program. The third type of supervision for school counselors is clinical, or counseling, supervision. A structured, though varying set of activities encouraging counselor self-awareness through feedback loops, counseling supervision can focus on skill enhancement, professional identity development, or other aspects of the school counselor's role in providing direct service to students. Unlike mental health counselors, school counselors usually receive little or no consistent counseling supervision.

Although evaluation is an important part of clinical supervision, it is not the only part (Borders, 1991). Principals are certainly qualified to evaluate school counselors in many ways, but they may not feel prepared to observe small group or individual counseling sessions and give helpful feedback on the process. While observation is needed in evaluation, the confidential nature of counseling interactions poses another ethical concern. Students' permission should be obtained before an individual or group counseling session is observed for evaluation and/or supervision purposes.

Clinical supervision is best provided by someone with counseling experience and training in the counseling supervision process. In a recent study (Crutchfield & Borders, 1997), the helpfulness of clinical supervision for school counselors (conducted by trained and experienced supervisors) was supported. School counselors who participated in this study reported that the supervision had provided them with both collegial support and skills acquisition. These participants reported feeling disappointed to see the supervision sessions end. In order for school counselors to receive adequate clinical supervision, outside supervisors, such as counselor educators or other professionals, may have to be consulted. Often counselor educators are willing to contract with school systems or individual school counselors to provide this counseling supervision for a minimal fee.

Another possible avenue for clinical supervision might be a peer consultation and supervision model (e.g., Benshoff & Paisley, 1996). Such structured models allow school counselors to meet together in dyads to provide support and to offer feedback on counseling skills. Of course, meeting together would be simplified if administrators were willing to allow school counselors some flexible release time to travel to another school and meet with other counselors for clinical supervision activities. Another means of administrative support might be hosting peer dyads or peer-group sessions at one's school. Because counseling supervision is not "built into" the school counselors job, it takes a great deal of flexibility and creativity to meet this particular professional development need.

Professional Associations

As previously mentioned, professional school counselors are often affiliated with ACA and ASCA, both national professional associations. ACA is the large umbrella professional association for all counseling professionals, and ASCA is the division of ACA for Professional School Counselors. Membership in these associations is often encouraged during school counselors' training programs. The benefits of membership include subscription to newsletters and professional refereed journals, catalogs with other resources such as books and videos, and reduced rates on professional liability insurance. These services are quite valuable and supply a ready means of professional development. Keeping up with the latest writings in the school counseling profession (through the professional journals) helps school counselors stay fresh, productive, and on the cutting edge in the field. In addition, ASCA supplies a School Counselor Role Statement and Position Statements on various salient topics as a guide for school counselors and administrators alike.

Some other professional associations that might interest school counselors include the Association for Specialists in Group Work (ASGW), the Association for Multicultural Counseling and Development (AMCD), the Association of Humanistic Education and Development (AHEAD), and the National Career Development Association (NCDA). All of these associations are divisions of ACA, and most have state chapters as well. Through these associations, listings of workshops and other professional development opportunities are often provided.

Conclusion

When school counselors receive appropriate professional development training, the outcomes may include continued professional and personal growth, professional accountability, and improved counseling effectiveness. More effective counselors can help produce higher academic performance and higher standardized test scores for their students. When it comes to professional development activities in the schools, there is often an overload of teacher-focused workshops. It would be a great help to school counselors if principals provided budget funds for counseling-specific professional development activities on an equal basis with those provided for other professionals. Opportunities for continued study, keeping up with current trends, addressing the changing needs of students, remaining aware of developing ethical issues, and ongoing clinical supervision are all appropriate avenues to professional school counselors' continued development.

In our search of the educational administration literature, we came across articles on the evaluation of school counselors, but nothing directly addressing clinical supervision or other school counseling professional issues. Research is needed to identify effective practices by principals regarding the supervision and professional development of school counselors, as well as the resolution of any conflicts between faculty or principals and counselors arising from ethical considerations.

References

American Association of School Administrators. (1976). *AASA Statement of ethics for school administrators and procedural guidelines.* Arlington, VA: Author.

American Counseling Association. (1995). *Ethical standards.* Alexandria, VA: Author.

American School Counselor Association. (1992). *Ethical standards for school counselors.* Alexandria, VA: Author.

Benshoff, J. M., & Paisley, P. O. (1996). The structured peer consultation model for school counselors. *Journal of Counseling and Development, 74,* 314-318.

Borders, L. D. (1991). Supervision-evaluation. *The School Counselor, 38,* 253-255.

Crutchfield, L. B., & Borders, L. D. (1997). Impact of two clinical peer supervision models on practicing school counselors. *Journal of Counseling and Development, 75,* 219-230.

Roberts, E. B., & Borders, L. D. (1994). Supervision of school counselors: Administrative, program, and counseling. *The School Counselor, 41,* 149-157.

Lori B. Crutchfield, Ph.D., NCSC, LPC is Assistant Professor and Coordinator of the School Counseling Program, Department of Counseling and Clinical Programs, Columbus State University, Columbus, GA.

Elizabeth S. Hipps, Ed.D. is Principal, Downtown Elementary Magnet School, a professional development school in Columbus, GA.

What a School Administrator Needs to Know About the Effectiveness Of School Counseling

Thomas Trotter, Gary Delka, & Susan Seaman

Introduction

Program evaluation is oftentimes viewed as an independent process conducted after the program has been established and is in operation. Rather, program evaluation should be treated as a fully integrated and continuous process by which data are gathered and decisions are made for the purpose of improving the program at critical points throughout its development. Such a process is available in an adaptation of Stufflebeam and Shinkfield's Context-Input-Process-Product (CIPP) model of evaluation (Trotter, 1992). Through this approach, school counseling programs are supported by a firm foundation established through comprehensive *context* evaluation undertaken to select and prioritize goals and target student competencies. *Context* evaluation activity is followed by a careful analysis of *inputs*, those activities and implementation strategies which have the potential to achieve identified goals and student competencies. As each step toward program improvement and development is taken, a *process* (or formative) evaluation of progress is conducted to monitor and revise chosen activities and strategies, as necessary. Finally, a *product* evaluation of outcomes is administered at the end of the school year to determine whether initially selected goals and competencies have been sufficiently accomplished through selected activities–as adjusted through *process* evaluation– to merit continuation, change, or termination.

Rationale

In advocating this improvement-oriented approach to program evaluation, the following premises are fundamental:

1. School counselors must be personally invested in the evaluation of their programs.
2. Program evaluation conducted at the front end of implementation is essential to determine the appropriateness of selected goals and student competencies which serve as the centerpiece to the school counseling program.
3. Evaluation is necessarily a many-faceted process which may include observations of certain behaviors, interviews, reviews of media productions and other records, focus group discussions, open forums or town hall meetings, formal surveys, standardized measures, and expert panel or peer reviews.
4. Program evaluation will be successful if endorsed by administrators, conducted by school counselors in collaboration with others, and honored by its many "customers."

Context Level Evaluation

The purpose of *context* level evaluation is to provide a rationale for counselors and administrators in choosing goals and student competencies, all of which help shape the program and highlight any structural elements in need of attention. It is here that evaluators must define the environment in which the program operates, identify any unmet needs, and determine why these needs are not being met. This evaluation is accomplished through a broad-based assessment of customer needs, a determination of current program strengths and weaknesses, and assignment of programming priorities.

Context level evaluation consists of four steps.

First, informally identify student needs through discussions with various customers (students, teachers, parents, et al.); review pertinent demographics (indices of poverty, attendance statistics, disciplinary proceedings); scan media productions for articles on children and youth; and access any other sources of information which might help structure formal evaluation activities. Analyze this input. Note specific unmet needs evident across the data. Referring to an established scope and sequence can help frame these elements.

Second, in constructing survey items, transform informally determined student needs to more formal assessment items suitable for inclusion, for interviewing representative customers, and for structuring open forums and focus group discussions. This step allows the school system to customize its needs assessment rather than borrowing instruments from other districts which would likely not reflect relevant needs or issues.

Third, to conduct a formal broad-based assessment of needs, distribute surveys, host focus groups comprised of representatives from customer groups, interview randomly selected customers, conduct expert panel or peer reviews, and convene open forums or town hall gatherings to which the public is invited and encouraged to provide input.

Fourth, in order to compare and contrast contemporary student needs with school counseling as currently practiced, conduct a time-and-task analysis of how school counselor time is presently expanded using a form like that advocated in Trotter's *Walking the Talk* (1991). Information should be collected over at least a month to ensure that data is representative of a typical day in the life of the school counselors.

Having collected information descriptive of local student needs and how school counseling time tends to be spent, evaluators are in a position to not only discern discrepancies between these two aspects but to help formulate school counseling goals and student competencies.

Input Level Evaluation

Input level evaluation is undertaken to help design the school counseling program. Armed with goals and competencies which reflect current student needs, school counselors are in a position to seek 'input' regarding best practices and programming strategies which address these goals. In addition, 'input' is sought as to how school system resources can be utilized to support chosen practices and strategies.

Programming options are explored through reviews of established curricula like Missouri's *Comprehensive Guidance Program*, Iowa's *Smoother Sailing Program*, and Connecticut's *K–12 Developmental Guidance and Counseling Program*. Also, evaluators are encouraged to consult with experts and successful practitioners, conduct literature reviews, visit operational programs, and peruse commercial catalogs for information regarding activities and strategies that work. Many publishers will allow potential users of materials to preview materials in advance of purchase. In an effort to assess system capabilities, evaluators are encouraged to inventory locally available human resources (school personnel, community professionals) for skills and expertise, sources of potential financial support (local, state, and national sources; private foundation funding), available equipment and material (computers, software, texts, furnishings), space, and political assets.

This inventory of resources can also be accomplished through what is referred to as the SWOT analysis. Usually associated with the strategic planning process, a SWOT analysis entails an assessment of strengths (S), weaknesses (W), opportunities (O), and threats (T). While identified weaknesses and threats pertain to *context* level evaluation and result in formulation of objectives, an analysis of strengths and opportunities relates more directly to *input* level evaluation because of its emphasis on both readily and potentially available resources (strengths and opportunities, respectively). These elements constitute planning strategies, the resources needed to implement the program.

Input level evaluation culminates in the development of action plans, each of which is built around an objective. Action plans contain information on strategies needed to achieve each objective, tactics needed to implement each strategy, person(s) responsible for implementing each tactic, resources needed, estimated time of tactic completion, and how accomplishment of each strategy will be measured.

Process Level Evaluation

Methods used to measure the extent to which each strategy is accomplished are detailed in the action plan. These methods constitute *process* level evaluation which is conducted to keep decision-makers informed as to how effectively priority goals and student competencies are being met. In addition, evaluation at this level is undertaken to help pinpoint any defects in selected activities and strategies. In this way, school counselors can make necessary mid-course corrections in programming rather than waiting until the program runs its course. At this point, it may be too late to make constructive changes.

Just as *context* level evaluation methods are many and varied, so too, are *process* level strategies. These may include pre-test and post-test measures of knowledge and skills, observations of selected student behaviors, self-reports of behavioral improvement, routine performance appraisal (grades, standardized test results, portfolios), ongoing self-studies, individual case studies, attendance and disciplinary data, and sociometric measures. It is also important to continue conducting "spot" time-and-task analyses to determine how actual expenditures of counselor time compare to standardized time prescriptions advocated through developmental school counseling.

Product Level Evaluation

As indicated, *process* level evaluation is conducted to provide ongoing feedback as to how effectively selected strategies address established goals. *Product* level evaluation usually resembles *context* level measures in content and enables evaluators to determine whether the program, as modified through *process* level evaluation, has succeeded in meeting initially identified needs-turned-goals and competencies. This level of evaluation also helps chart a course for future action. To this end, the *product* level evaluation serves as next year's *context* evaluation. Additionally, outcomes of evaluation at this level stand as a record of accomplishment regarding practices which worked, provide direction regarding areas in need of improvement, shed light on the effectiveness of the evaluation model to aid decision making, reinforce efforts of faculty and staff, and may help secure necessary support for program continuance.

Product level methods might include the same survey administered as a component of the *context* evaluation. Additional sources of input might include customer feedback, peer and expert panel review, focus group discussions, interviews with selected customers, an end-of-the-year open forum, and reviews of student attendance and disciplinary information.

Conclusion

Evaluation is a continuous process by which data are gathered and decisions are made for the purpose of developing and improving a program. Thorough evaluation is essential to success in school counseling. An adaptation of the CIPP approach accomplishes both of these goals by offering a systematic, integrated approach to program development. Through this model, each step in the process builds on the outcomes of the preceding step (Trotter, 1992). Needs-based goals are developed through *context* evaluation, goal-driven activities are identified and committed to action planning through <u>input</u> measures, *process* level evaluation is conducted to monitor activities as they are implemented, and finally, *product* evaluation is undertaken to determine the overall impact of the school counseling program to address needs-based goals which were formulated at the front end of program development and improvement.

References

Stufflebeam, D. L., & Shinkfield, A. J. (1985). *Systematic evaluation.* Boston, MA: Kluwer-Nijhoff Publishing.

Trotter, T. V. (1991). *Walking the talk—Developing a local comprehensive school counseling program.* Alexandria, VA: American School Counselor Association.

Trotter, T. V. (1992). *A developmental model of evaluation for developmental school counseling programs.* Boise, ID: Idaho Division of Vocational Education.

Thomas V. Trotter, Ph.D., is Associate Professor, Counseling and School Psychology, University of Idaho, Moscow, ID.

Gary G. Delka, Ed.D., is Associate Professor, Education Administration, University of Idaho, Moscow, ID.

Susan Seaman, Ed.S., is Curriculum Director, School District No. 271, Moscow, ID.

What a School Administrator Needs to Know About *Religious and Political Challenges School Counseling*

Rolla E. Lewis & Mary Beth VanCleave

Religion and politics both emerge from deeply held values. These values reveal central assumptions about what we believe metaphysically and about what we want from our government. Because these values are so emotionally charged, they fall prey to simplistic good-bad, black-white, dualistic arguments that frequently lead to destructive positions that allow the loudest or largest group to prevail without respecting other points of view. Clearly, there are no convergent answers to religious truths and political perspectives, so counselors must call all members of the school community to be tolerant and sensible.

Values and School Counseling

Religious and political values frequently define boundaries and distinctions within a community, and school counselors are in a position to work with all members of the community. At the same time, school counselors have their own personal and professional values. They are not detached, neutral observers. Every person swims in individual, family, and cultural values, and the counseling profession is willing to admit this reality. Rather than deny the existence or influence of values, counselors go to great lengths to be explicit about their professional values and to develop awareness of how their personal values influence their work with others— especially others with values differing from the counselor. Christopher (1996) states, "Ultimately counseling is part of a cultural discussion about ethos and world view, about the good life and the good person, and about moral visions" (p. 24). Broadly speaking, counseling is permeated with ethics. According to Baker (1996), the school guidance and school counseling profession emerged as a response to the exploitation and ill-use of people. School counselors have the ability to become the professional conscience in the communities they serve by focusing on social reform within public school systems and by teaching democratic values and behaviors to those they serve.

Baker (1996) calls for the school counseling profession to nurture social reform. And, indeed, that is exactly what school counseling does as it continues to address numerous social problems such as teen pregnancy, suicide, decline of the traditional two-parent family, working parents, AIDS, dramatic changes in the economy, and the stability of the workplace (Baker, 1996). In addition, school counseling continues to strive for equity and understanding among the wide-variety of political and religious groups found in our society. Differences found in culture, race, gender, physical ability, and intellectual capacity are opportunities to expand our understanding of ourselves as individuals and as a society (Baker, 1996). Social justice and social reform are integral to the school counseling profession because school counselors are guided by principles that promote individual growth, social development, and appreciation of differences.

Ethical Standards and Legal Issues for School Counselors

The Ethical Standards for School Counselors (ASCA, 1992) are embedded in a tradition linked to democratic principles and individual rights. It is also true, however, that such principles which focus on the individual may run counter to the religious and political values held by parents. For instance, the act of teaching decision-making during school guidance and counseling activities may threaten certain parents who want their children to "act obediently to the higher authority of parents or religion"

(Kaplan, 1996, p. 166).

In the case of school counselors working with strongly religious families, it is critical to be sensitive to the beliefs guiding the family. For example, Christian fundamentalist parents may be apprehensive and fearful about the counseling process because they believe that misbehavior reflects a spiritually based problem. Miller (1995) points out that such parents are concerned that the counselor will ignore (a) their spiritual concerns; (b) not understand their beliefs or concerns; (c) assume that the family shares standards of many non-religious parents; (d) recommend behaviors and solutions they consider immoral; and (e) doubt the usefulness of what the family has learned through prayer. To help school counselors address these concerns, Miller (1995) offers the following guidelines (a) be honest and up front with your values when working with these families; (b) recognize and validate their religious experience and perspective; (c) seek their help in understanding their position; (d) do not challenge the family's religious authority; (e) recognize that access to divergent information may be limited for the family; and (f) consider making a referral if necessary. This protocol can be extended to any number of relationships that deal with political or religious concerns. In those cases where the political and religious values of either individuals or the community conflict with the values guiding the school counselor, school counselors should be sure to educate school administrators on the key issues surrounding those conflicts. Moreover, the school administrator should be made aware of the protocols which school counselors are ethically bound to follow.

School Counseling and Challenging Topics

Confidentiality is a key value for counselors. School counselors adhere to the principle of confidentially with students by keeping what students say during counseling sessions confidential within the limits of the law. To a large extent, the law is clear about the counselor's duty to warn and his or her duty to protect clients. For example, if a student expresses suicidal thoughts, parents would be contacted and every effort made to ensure that the student receives necessary care and support.

If a student shares information about sexual activity or pregnancy, more challenging religious and political issues are raised. In many instances, depending upon state laws and local policies, a counselor might or might not be required to contact the parents. Because laws and board policies vary from state to state and from district to district, there is room for ethical and legal discussion. Birth control and pregnancy are two highly charged religious and political topics. A school counselor might inform students about the availably of birth control methods and refer students to family planning or health clinics for more information. In a similar vein, a school counselor's knowledge of a pregnancy and a student's possible decision to have an abortion brings the national debate between right-to-life and pro-choice forces right into the school and might prompt different and equally ethical actions by different counselors. One counselor might encourage a student to discuss pregnancy with her parents, whereas another counselor might refer a student to a family planning or health clinic without informing the parents. Depending on the circumstances, the same counselor might make a decision one way with one counselee and another way with another counselee. The critical point for the counselor would be to know the difference between imposing personal views on the student and providing information. Judgment in such cases is not easy. Counselors must know about the range of local agencies that provide help for pregnant youth, and make every effort to find the student a good support system to prevent the student from harming herself. Clearly, any decision must be informed by relevant laws, school board policies, and the social value that parents have the primary responsibility for raising children. At the same time, numerous other variables, including the student's safety, might influence the counselor's professional judgment.

Professional judgment is the critical variable in encountering religious and political issues for school counselors. For instance, the extent to which a gay or lesbian youth might attract attention if he or she "came out" is dependent on that young person's community. In one community, such a public proclamation might be greeted with acceptance, in another community with physical violence. Because same-gender sexual orientation is a charged religious and political topic, administrators who defer to a school counselor's judgment might offer the most effective way to help the child. In taking on this responsibility, counselors must be aware of their own views and the possible need to refer a student to someone else. The counselor will be faced with dealing with a number of issues including looking at the consequences for coming out or being engaged in same-gender behavior. For example, the student might evoke anger and rage from his family, be told to leave his home, lose friends, or be physically assaulted. If sexually active, the student needs to know about safe sex. In general, the counselor must help gay and lesbian students assess the level of homophobia within the community and to help the student assess the level of care and support that will be sacrificed by coming out.

Providing a setting for students to explore such issues may cause certain members of the community to view the counselor as condoning the "sin" of homosexuality. Because over 70% of AIDS cases are due to same-gender sexual contact or intravenous drug use, AIDS has been described by some as resulting from "sinful behavior." Over 22% of those with AIDS are in their twenties, and many were infected while they were still in school (Gibson & Mitchell, 1995). This alarming statistic makes clear the vital role that school counselors play in informing students about the disease and the psychological reactions that occur for those with the disease. Just as an ethical school counselor would confront racism within the organizations they work, school counselors are encouraged to take steps to educate for greater compassion, tolerance, and sensibility in the community concerning health issues.

Counselors in a School Community

The political and religious challenges to school counseling require that administrators understand the necessity to develop a comprehensive counseling plan that allows school counselors a flexible and professional response to difficult problems. By respecting different beliefs and by soliciting information from a wide spectrum of groups within their community, the North Clackamas School District (in Oregon) has been able to develop policies regarding religious beliefs and customs that are respectful of the varied beliefs and traditions in the community. The policy provides teachers, counselors, and site administrators guidelines for creating a community that encourages tolerance, understanding, and sensibility (North Clackamas School District, 1995).

Another area school administrators must consider is the Family Educational Rights and Privacy Act (i.e., Buckley Amendment). Although the Buckley Amendment is primarily a guide to student records and related activities, there are political and religious considerations which impact school counseling. Counselors could face defamation suits from students or parents who have gained access to counseling files and who believe comments contained there are libelous. For example, describing children as being members of a "cult" may be libelous. Given the scope of the Buckley Amendment, counselors would be wise to avoid placing such descriptive statements in students' records.

Overall, it is extremely prudent for school administrators to develop written policies or guidelines for school counselors that have been reviewed by experienced school counselors, clinicians, and lawyers. Because school counselors are called to serve the entire community, districts that are explicit about their values help counselors to understand and respond effectively to political and religious challenges within the context of that community. School counselors are in a position to point out that, when it comes to religion and politics, there are multiple perspectives about what to believe and how to govern, and these perspectives need to be treated with tolerance and sensitivity in order to maintain an effective democracy.

References

American School Counselor Association. (1992). *Ethical standards for school counselors.* Alexandria, VA: Author.

Baker, S. B. (1996). *School counseling for the twenty-first century.* Englewood Cliffs, NJ: Merrill.

Christopher, J. C. (1996). Counseling's inescapable moral visions. *Journal of Counseling and Development, 75,* 17-25.

Gibson, R. L., & Mitchell, M. H. (1995). *Introduction to counseling and guidance.* Englewood Cliffs, NJ: Merrill.

Kaplan, L. S. (1996). Outrageous or legitimate concerns: What some parents are saying about school counseling. *The School Counselor, 43,* 165-170.

Miller, D. R. (1995). The school counselor and Christian fundamentalist families. *The School Counselor, 42,* 317-321.

North Clackamas School District. (1995). *Questions/answers-religious beliefs and customs.* Milwaukie, OR: North Clackamas School District.

Rolla E. Lewis, Ed.D., is Assistant Professor in Counseling and Curriculum & Instruction at Portland State University in Portland, Oregon.

Mary Beth VanCleave, Ph.D., is the Principal of Kelly Elementary School, a nationally recognized Basic School in Portland, Oregon.

What a School Administrator Needs to Know About What School Administrators Can Do to Promote School Counseling

John W. Bloom & George Davidson

Overview

We hope that this collaborative effort between a professor of educational administration and a professor of counselor education will serve as a model for cooperation between school administrators and guidance counselors. The writers of this capsule are advocates of building a community of leadership based on expert and referent power in which both counselor and administrator acknowledge a willingness to follow the other out of respect for the person and her wisdom. With expert and referent power administrators automatically will follow many of the suggestions in the first list, while avoiding those in the second.

Things That Make School Counselors SOAR!

1. Expecting accountability while providing resources to accomplish the same will increase communication between counselor and administrator (Schmidt, 1993).
2. Helping counselors develop an annual assessment and growth plan based on counseling knowledge and skills

rather than teacher knowledge and skills (Schmidt, 1993).

3. Asking guidance counselors about technological advancements that can be integrated to make their work more efficient.

4. Asking counselors which conferences they would like to attend and providing appropriate financial support from the district.

5. Asking counselors when National School Counseling Week is and what you can do to help with the observance. Better yet, call the American School Counselor Association yourself at (800) 306-4722.

6. Understanding that counselors need time for reflection. They often are bombarded with the need to make critical decisions impacting students' welfare at every turn. Does this student get placed in special education? Does that student get placed in a residential treatment center? Does this student get recommended for the Air Force Academy? Does that parent get reported for child abuse? Does this teacher need emotional assistance after experiencing a personal tragedy? Helping counselors take care of themselves makes them better helpers of others!

7. Recognizing your counselors publicly. For example, the Indiana Middle Level Education Association recognizes the outstanding middle level educator, counselor and administrator of the year, not just the outstanding teacher of the year.

8. Inviting your counselors to make a presentation to your professional association (e.g., National Association of Secondary School Principals, American Association of School Boards, American Association of School Administrators.).

9. Making sure that your school and district's goals reflect a commitment to meeting the educational, career, and personal social needs of all students. This is what counselors are all about.

10. Encourage and support, with time and money, your

counselors to obtain professional credentials such as the National Certified School Counselor credential from the National Board for Certified Counselors which is a more rigorous credential review process than that of most state departments of education (Clawson, 1993).

11. Using counselor's expertise as group facilitators to lead parent discussion groups at PTO meetings, faculty retreats, etc.

12. Ask your counselor to discuss the American School Counselor Association and the American Counseling Association Code of Ethics with you over lunch. You both need to know what parameters govern each other's professions (Remley, 1993).

13. Giving guidance counselors more autonomy to make decisions reduces dependence on administrators and increases counselors' esteem.

Things That Make School Counselors SORE!

1. Only talking about teachers and administrators when talking about your "wonderful staff."

2. Counselors aren't "shrinks." In fact they are "stretches" who help students, parents, teachers, and administrators think beyond the confines of "the box."

3. Touchy-Feely is so "sixties"! Don't use it to describe your counselors.

4. Not respecting counselors' or students' privacy and confidentiality needs.

5. Asking your counselor to perform mundane administrative or secretarial tasks or substitute or supervision (lunchroom, school busses, etc.). Don't ask counselors to do bad things to students and then expect them to do good things.

6. Failing to provide adequate facilities, equipment, and resources for counseling and guidance. Some believe that because counseling involves talk, that there are no consumables needed. Promote

counseling by adopting a realistic budget for your counseling staff.

7. Chaining your counselors to endless paperwork that could be done more efficiently by hourly staff at less cost.

8. Hiring a new school counselor without input from current school counseling staff (see Dykeman chapter). Encourage the hiring of individuals who possess proper professional credentials.

9. Hiring uncredentialed people when credentialed professionals are available. Doing so indicates a disrespect of the credentials already held by the counseling staff. And remember that in most states the standard is for counselors to have completed 48 semester hour programs in school counseling.

10. Ridiculing your counselors for being so sensitive!

11. Letting counselors get bogged down in excessive special education assessments, staffings and report writings, all of which inhibit their ability to work with all students.

12. Jeopardizing the entire staff by not having a widely publicized, legally defensible, written plan for dealing with traumatic incidents and emergencies on campus.

13. Expecting counselors to provide Employee Assistant Program services for impaired faculty and staff when they don't have adequate time to work with students.

Conclusion

What happens when school administrators become spokespersons for the school counseling profession and those highly trained counseling and guidance professionals in their buildings? Former Indiana Middle School Administrator of the Year, Herbert Bunch, has his likeness appended to a card that says, "It's amazing what you can accomplish when you don't care who gets the credit."

References

Clawson, T. (1993). The school counselor and credentialing. In J. Wittmer (Ed.), *Managing your school counseling program*. Minneapolis, MN: Educational Media Corp.

Remley, T. (1993). Legal and ethical issues in school counseling. In J. Wittmer (Ed.), *Managing your school counseling program*. Minneapolis, MN: Educational Media Corp.

Schmidt, J. (1993). Counselor accountability: Justifying your time and measuring your worth. In J. Wittmer (Ed.), *Managing your school counseling program*. Minneapolis, MN: Educational Media Corp.

John W. Bloom, Ph.D., NCC, NCSC is Coordinator of the Counselor Education Program, Butler University, Indianapolis, IN.

George Davidson, Ph.D., is Associate Professor, Educational Administration, Butler University, Indianapolis, IN.

Summary

Cass Dykeman, Series Editor

From Herr's "Introduction" to Bloom and Davidson's closing capsule, this series has sought to enhance your knowledge of school counseling. The capsule authors and I hope that this increased knowledge will generate in you a new confidence and energy to participate in your school counseling program. Your leadership can make a big difference in how well school counselors serve parents, teachers, and students!